# Zen and the Mind

# ZEN AND THE MIND

## *Scientific Approach to Zen Practice*

by Tomio Hirai, M.D.

Japan Publications, Inc.

© 1978 BY TOMIO HIRAI

*Published by*
JAPAN PUBLICATIONS, INC., TOKYO

*Distributed by*
JAPAN PUBLICATIONS TRADING COMPANY
200 Clearbrook Road, Elmsford, N. Y. 10523, U.S.A.
1174 Howard Street, San Francisco, Calif. 94103, U.S.A.
P.O. Box 5030 Tokyo International, Tokyo 101–31, Japan

First edition: April 1978

*ISBN 0–87040–391–5*

Printed in Japan by Kyodo Printing Co., Ltd.

# Preface

In recent years, psychological and neurophysiological studies on altered states of consciousness have been focused on the understanding of the relations between brain mechanisms and consciousness in general. Such studies have given rise to attempts to relate various neurophysiological findings with psychological states and behavioral correlates. Among research in this field, two trends are recognizable.

The first trend is research aimed at explaining changes in consciousness brought about by hypnosis, autogenic training, Yoga meditation, and transcendental meditation. Studies of this kind have concentrated on both mental and physical relaxation of the human mind. For example, autogenic training has been used in treating various neurotic states and psychosomatic ailments; and Raja Yoga is often used to obtain the kind of mental relaxation that accompanies psychophysiological changes.

The second trend involves voluntary control using the method of operant conditioning. This well-designed scientific method has produced good results in terms of behavioral and autonomic reactions in both animals and human beings.

Operant conditioning leads to the study of relations between regulation of bodily processes and consciousness. Various people have advanced various terms to describe the mechanism whereby such changes are brought about. Niel E. Miller (1969) calls it the result of control. Joe Kamiya (1971) calls it biofeedback; and David Shapiro et al. (1969) have described it as self-control. All of these terms indicate the existence of a control system with innate potentialities that can be manifested through training or learning on the part of the organism itself.

In the past few years, scholars and doctors of both psychology and medicine have been showing keen interest in Zen meditation. Practice of Zen meditation is said to emancipate man from the dualistic bondage of subjectivity and objectivity of mind and body. By being awakened to the pure, serene self, the person is freed of lust and self-consciousness. The state of mind produced by this emancipation is called *satori* (enlightenment) and is the true nature of the human being.

For about twenty years, my colleagues and I have been studying the psychological and physiological aspects of the mental and physical states that occur during Zen meditation, one of the methods employed for the sake of attaining enlightenment. The result of our work is the assertion that Zen meditation is more than Zen Buddhist training since it influences the body as well as the mind. Scientifically it can be shown that Zen meditation regulates the whole organism of the body internally and externally. How this is done is the material of this book. Here I want only to say that Zen meditation is a useful training method for relaxing the mind and enabling the individual to realize his true self.

In an earlier work on this subject—*Zen Meditation Therapy*, which is the English-language version of a Japanese-language original—I touched on some aspects of the subject. But, wanting to expand and deepen my treatment of this important topic, I decided to produce this wide-scale, scientific explanation of our findings and of the exact method used in Zen meditation.

I should like to close these brief remarks by saying that Zen is a rich source of emancipation from the severe social conditions of modern times for the layman as well as for the priest. It can be of immense value to all mankind.

February, 1978

TOMIO HIRAI

# Contents

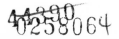

# Introduction

People from other countries often say that the Japanese are too industrious. I suspect that all of my readers, no matter where they are or where they may go, will someday have a chance to meet Japanese businessmen or to observe the way they work. A friend of mine who was studying in the United States related to me the following experience, which sheds some light on the Japanese attitude toward work and the ways other people can interpret it. One day, when he had just begun his stay in America, he decided to go to the university laboratory on Sunday to continue some research but was stopped by the gate guard, who asked him why he was there and where he intended to go. Though my friend explained that he wanted to spend some time performing an experiment in the laboratory, the guard refused to believe him. Only when my friend presented his identification card with his photograph on it and explained his purpose once again did the guard finally allow him to pass, but not without making the following remark: "Hey you! We've only got a few of your kind around here; they're mostly nuts. Better watch out!"

According to some sociologists, wherever man lives, there is work. According to others, wherever man lives, there is leisure and play. Both viewpoints are valid. At the risk of offending dog and cat fanciers, who claim practically human attributes for their pets, I think I can safely say that no other animal reacts to work and play the way man does. I do not deny the anthropologists' claim that other animals engage in both kinds of activities. I do say, however, that only in man have work and play been strongly and deeply connected since ancient times.

In modern civilization, the relation between the two has taken on a different aspect. A rift has occurred between man the laborer (*homo economicus*) and man the player (*homo ludens*). Though this tendency is by no means a good one, modern civilization seems to be unable to do anything but aggravate the dichotomy. This phenomenon is certainly related to the urbanization of the population and widespread industrialization prevalent in Japan and most other parts of the world.

Ancient Japanese festivals illustrate the way in which work and play were formerly tightly connected in the minds of the people. When the grain harvest was in, people held autumnal festivals to give thanks for the crop of that year and to express hopes for a good crop the coming year. The festivals embodied both the continuity of work and play of agricultural peoples and an essentially unchanging human desire for prosperity. Now all of this has altered. Autumnal festivals in many districts of Japan have lost their original basic meaning and have been turned into tourist attractions, and many of them are controlled by the leisure industries. They are now articles of production for financial profit. And the tendency to convert traditional festivals into commercial attractions has for some time been growing stronger throughout the world. Play becomes the prey of the leisure industry. This does not mean that people who go through with festivals do not find such occasions entertaining. In fact, Japanese workers continue to earn the money to maintain expenditures on this kind of leisure. But clearly there is a tendency for the split between work and play to be deepened and widened by the element of profit introduced by the leisure industries.

From this I draw a conclusion. The heart of our current dilemma is not such things as multiplicity of values, crisis of identity, or loss of a sense of existence. I believe that the core of the issue is to be found in the difficulty man experiences when he tries to lead a bifurcated daily life.

Where can the true human being seek help in such a situation? If neither work nor play any longer has value for human existence or in connection with emotional longings, perhaps dependence on alcohol is the answer. In his book *On Drink,* Kingsley Amis says that an American investigation team has stated the opinion that, if alcohol did not act simultaneously as a relaxant and a goad, at about the time of World War I, Western Society would have collapsed irrevocably. Maybe something similar could be said about Japanese society at the present time.

At least it is certain that the traditional one drink after work tastes delicious. It has the effect of linking daily life with the rhythm of fun and in this way avoids the stresses of human relations and the split between work and play. For this reason, people have long cherished this tradition. The drink tastes good because the person having it lives a life in which work and play are part of the same unified stream of true humanity.

In difficult modern circumstances, when the alcohol is consumed as a way of overcoming the rift between work and play, it does not taste as good. Work today often involves all kinds of parties: luncheons, dinners, cocktail parties, and so on. Willy-nilly, strangers, uncertain whether they are supposed to be working or amusing themselves, gather in rooms where the only consistently offered thing is a wide variety of alcoholic beverages. In the old days, social gatherings consisted of acquaintances, all from a social unit probably no larger than a village. Today, at parties, one must chat with crowds of strangers. Those attending these parties suffer from anxiety, insecurity, and fear of strangers because they do not know what to discuss with each other. Alcohol is the only thing that can break down the walls separating partygoers. On such occasions, it acts as a kind of tranquilizer to alleviate unnecessary suffering.

But this kind of drinking is an allopathic, not a cure. Once a person becomes accustomed to it, he turns to drink, even when alone, as a way of getting rid of mental anxiety. This kind of person has what is called the alcohol-dependent mentality. It is no coincidence that alcoholism is becoming an increasingly grave problem in the advanced nations. Antagonism among the members of society, arising as does the separation of work and play, is the cause of the increasing dependence on alcohol. Bacchus has lost his appeal and charm. He has been transformed into a road to hell, in the shape of chronic alcoholism.

A famous explorer has said that thirst is more terrible than hunger. In the material overabundance of the advanced nations, hunger is no longer a serious problem for most people. But mankind is mentally desiccated. Our society is a jungle of materialistic trees of kinds found in no primeval groves. The inhabitants of the jungle are in need of an overflowing pure, clear fountain. We all eat too much; it is as if the leaves of a chocolate tree fell ready into our hands whenever we wanted them. But we are increasingly in need of something to quench our spiritual thirst. Man today has either lost or is losing the clear spring of the mind itself.

Beneath superficial flourishing, our cities are asphalt jungles; their citizens are desert creatures. From somewhere on the distant horizon, the forces of work are marshaled against us. From separate quarters, the powers of play drive down on us. Still worse, people, looking just like us but actually strangers or even alien creatures, assault us one by one, inspiring us with anxiety and insecurity. Gradually, without being aware of what is happening, we find ourselves in a realm of suffering.

Not only has modern man lost the road to salvation, he has also fallen into something like "criminal ways" involving drug addiction, deliquency, and so on. Indicative of this trend was the April, 1977, edition of the American magazine *Newsweek*, which was dedicated to the topic "Heroine Invades Europe." On the other hand, in Japan, neurotic behavior is on the increase. For instance, among the middle rank of management businessmen, melancholia is becoming common. Adolescents develop what might be called school-phobia. Housewives become hypochondriac. Elderly people must often drag themselves through gray days, unlightened by any reason for living. As the newspapers constantly report, many people behave in odd ways without actually displaying neuroses. Relations between labor and management continue to deteriorate; and a gloomy, heavy air has begun to pervade our society, in spite of the steady growth of places of amusement where, at least on the surface, everything is lively and cheery. In a recent edition of a medical journal, a psychiatrist reported a growing number of neurotic-apathetic Oblomov-like high-school and college students. Police reports tell of juvenile delinquency, addiction to sniffing paint thinner, murder resulting from the abuse of stimulant drugs, prostitution among middle-school girls, and inexplicable suicides among young people. Surely such facts tell of an age closed in on itself, an age that has lost the way to salvation. The surface glitter of our world is no more than white-wash on the tomb. Under the paint lurks the dark, slimy cause of human spiritual decay.

Psychiatrists are deeply interested in questions like where should I work and what kind of work should I do? Or is it absolutely essential that I find some kind of amusement for the sake of mental health? When pressed or irritated, people seek temporary relief from mental thirst in superficial brilliance and abundance.

Of course, alcohol, sedatives, narcotics, and stimulant drugs are not wisdom at all. They are conducive to the ruin, not to the salvation, of life. They may suffice for people who interpret wisdom as no more than ease and comfort, free of suffering and pain. But such ease is inevitably short-lived.

I am convinced that people today have lost the understanding of the true meaning of life wisdom, just as they have lost an understanding of true salvation. The guarantee of ease and material security does not necessarily ensure happiness. Perhaps man today pursues the materially rich life too assiduously. The recent oil shock and energy crisis have flashed a warning signal to the effect that the easy life will be in danger in the future. At present, scientists in all field are attempting to work out solutions for the serious problems facing man in the twenty-first century, especially food shortages caused by drastic increases in world population.

We have reached a branching point in the current of history: one stream leads to a search for salvation and relief for man's spiritual desiccation; the other leads to the search for solutions to real daily problems and to ways to avoid the material crisis of the future. The two currents do not contradict each other. They flow together to whirl and billow as the main tide of our times. Psychologists, psychiatrists, economists, sociologists, and scientists in other. fields are now issuing warnings, solution proposals, and other propositions for the sake of rediscovering both salvation and practical life wisdom.

Many times before in history, mankind has been buffeted by similar whirlpools and has been put in physical and mental danger. Each time man has overcome the crisis, he has been able to build a new age and a new, hope-filled way of life.

Zen meditation has the power to save from mental crises and to prevent man from being tossed and washed away by the tide of the age. The explanation of how it has such an effect is the main theme of this book. But before turning to that subject, I must outline the course of events by means of which Zen came into being.

Born in ancient India as a prince in a small tribe, Siddhartha Gautama, who was to become the Buddha, the Enlightened One, left his father's home and his wife and child, because he had become aware of the transience of all human life. Though it is not known how he came to this awareness, it is possible to make a reasonable guess. Located in the monsoon belt, India experiences yearly typhoons, droughts, and floods. The climatic conditions of the land are cruel; and, in the Buddha's time, death must have been something that countless people faced daily. Under such circumstances, the transience of life must have been obvious.

The many religions—including, of course, Brahmanism—of the Indians of more than two thousand years ago, when the Buddha was born, were all regarded as ways to salvation. The sages and philosophers taught salvation in various guises. Before he began meditiation under a pipal tree and ultimately attained enlightenment, the Buddha probably listened to the teachings of many of these men and drew upon them in the development of his own philosophy. But none of the teachings of any single group satisfied him. He was less concerned with death as the cause of the transience of life than with the search for a way of experiencing peace and tranquility in the limited amount of lifetime allotted to the human being.

After extended meditation under a pipal tree, suddenly enlightenment burst upon him with the brilliance of the light of the morning star; and he became the Buddha, the Enlightened One, the one who has attained the highest state. He entered the realm of Nirvana, free of all such irrelevances as illness, suffering, aging, and death.

According to tradition, the Indian priest Bodhidharma brought Zen teachings to China in 520 of the Christian Era. From the end of the sixth to the beginning of the seventh century, a number of famous Chinese priests carried on his teachings. At the time, the nation was torn by warring and strife; and the people lacked mental security. Buddhist priests offered Zen teachings to the people as a way to satisfy their longing for salvation and made further spiritual progress themselves by pursuing the deeper meanings of Zen. Through their efforts, a Zen very different from what Bodhidharma had introduced into China was born. The learned priests vigorously advocated Zen Buddhism as a way of bringing security to the masses.

But it seems that they concentrated their efforts more on preaching than on practical activity. The highly intellectual and spiritually advanced priests taught a doctrine of *mu*, or nothingness, which was a state into which they sought to escape from the conflicts of their times. But the result was a defeatist kind of enlightenment that had lost contact with the ordinary affairs of actuality. These men had reasons for adopting this policy, but as time passed and political leaders restored peace to the land, the always practical Chinese lost interest in theories of nothingness and difficult abstract philosophy. Zen, then, arose during a time of great national trouble in China, gained popularity during the T'ang dynasty (618–906), flourished under the Sung dynasty (960–1279), and gradually declined under the succeeding Yüan (Mongol) dynasty (1280–1368).

Though the final fall did not come until about the thirteenth century, trouble had started much earlier. One cause was the conflict between Buddhism and Confucianism, which had played an important role in Chinese affairs from very ancient times and which was in harmony with the general Chinese practicality. With the passing of time, Confucianism swallowed Buddhism up and drastically altered its viewpoint. Buddhism had taught that we should let the world be as it is since it is all relative and unimportant. Confucianism taught that we should leave the world as it is because it is perfectly ordered and requires no changing. By the time this philosophy had been incorporated into Buddhism, the mission of Chinese Zen was finished.

The other cause of the downfall of Zen and other Buddhist sects in China was persecution. During the Northern Chou dynasty (557–581), the reluctance of Zen monks to recognize the authority of anything but the Buddhist teachings aroused the anger of the emperor Wu (543–576), who exiled many and executed others. To escape persecution in this age and later in the Sung period, some of the most famous Chinese Buddhist monks fled to Japan. They had two reasons for selecting this destination.

In the first place, Japanese monks studying in China had asked Chinese priests to share their wisdom, the usefulness of which the Japanese appreciated especially in that time when their home-land was suffering from famine, plagues, and internal strife. Furthermore Japanese priests had constantly sought physical and mental restoration in Chinese Zen teachings. In the second place, the Chinese monks knew that the efforts of Japanese priests in their homeland had prepared the way for an acceptance of Zen Buddhism. The persecution of Buddhist monks in China and consequent emigrations to Japan continued for about six hundred years.

The political situation in Japan in the late twelfth and thirteenth centuries provided refuge for Chinese monks. The wars between the Minamoto and Taira clans had ended with a Minamoto victory in 1185. Minamoto no Yoritomo, who had become the shogun, or military ruler of the land, established his government (shogunate) in a town called Kamakura, not far from modern Tokyo. A major element in his political policy was to sponsor calm among the people for the sake of the security of the social structure. Yoritomo apparently welcomed Zen priests to his city because he felt—perhaps mistakenly—that their teachings had played a role in establishing stability in China. It seems convincing, however, that he and other politicians sought emotional calm and relief from the difficulties of their daily work and life in Zen teachings and meditation. The biography of Minamoto no Yoritomo clearly indicates that he thought this way, and the temples that still survive in Kamakura bear witness to the amounts of time, effort, and money devoted to providing suitable establishments for Zen priests.

Though in this period the military government controlling the country had set itself up in Kamakura, the imperial court in Kyoto remained the source of legitimacy of the shogunate. Though deprived of practical power, the emperor was nonetheless the ritual head of the land and, as such, received a degree of deference. The lot of the emperors was by no means easy, and they no doubt found solace in the teachings of Japanese Zen priests who had studied on the continent. Still they must have realized that what such men told them was no more than a part of the total picture. For this reason, they welcomed Chinese priests who immigrated into Japan.

For these men, large temples were built in Kyoto—many of them still stand. At the temples, the emperors probably found counsel and comfort from the problems of their daily lives. In modern terms, Zen priests and their temples constituted virtual psychiatric counseling departments.

But it was not merely for their own spiritual stability that the leaders of the times requested aid from Zen. Both the Kamakura shogun and the emperor in Kyoto faced the imperative need of ensuring the spiritual calm and security of the entire populace. They therefore encouraged and gave economic protection to immigrant Chinese Zen priests. And it was only natural that Japanese priests should flock around these men to learn the theories and actual practices of Zen. In their search, they did not regard religious teaching and practical activity or salvation and daily-life wisdom as opposed dualities. Instead, they assumed the practical viewpoint that was to be found the truth of enlightenment both aspects of the duality. They hoped to find total happiness in thought, feeling, and action from this true enlightenment.

The two most representative figures in the history of Zen in

Japan are Dōgen (1200–1253), the founder of the Sōtō sect, and Keizan (1267–1325), the founder of the Soji-ji, one of the most important temples of the Sōtō sect. These two men established the course that Zen was to follow. Though Dōgen was more a theoretician and Keizan a man of a more practical turn of mind, their influences have harmonized to produce unity of theory and practice. In doing this, they laid the foundation for Japanese Zen and enabled it to blossom, take root, and remain strong to the present day.

Modern Zen is not a religion offering only spiritual help; it does not attempt to captivate the mind with mysticism and abstruse philosophy. As the priests of the past knew, it provides the mental and physical well being that man in all ages requires. I have proved this scientifically and feel it my duty to explain what I have learned to others.

# Meditation for Modern Man

## 1. The Nature of Neuroses

We psychiatrists, who come into contact with many patients suffering from neuroses, have a general impression of stress and anxiety that, though difficult to explain in concrete terms, can be roughly described in the following way. People with such conditions shrug their shoulders constantly, have tense facial expressions, allow their gazes to wander, and give an overall impression of tension. Their mood of suffering conveys itself to people who associate with them. The tension they experience is unlike the excitement of stage fright. Sometimes even people who are outwardly healthy and vigorous show signs of lack of mental flexibility and an inability to be calm.

The victim of neuroses is dominated by frustrations and insecurities that have persisted for a long time and are likely to continue into the future because he makes no attempt to solve them for himself. Unable to restrain or escape from the unpleasantness that torments his mind, the neurotic finds himself in a dead-end street from which there is no turning back. He is like a lost child, and his mental suffering finds physical symbolization in such symptoms as dizziness, palpitations, headaches, stiff shoulders, weakness, and fatigue. In other words, his loss of mental resilience finds pathological expression.

Without actually becoming neurotic, many of us fall into a state not far from neurosis. Tensions and anxiety similar to the kinds that bring on neurosis can be seen in the crowds of people who, no matter whether busy or idle, are fidgety, restless, and irritable;

who breathe short and fast; and who walk the streets with eyes glued to the ground. Subconsciously increasing frustrations, insecurities, and desires can turn us into mentally lost children. All kinds of desires pursue mankind. Perhaps sexual drives and greed are among the less harmful ones. Such manifestations of destructive drives as the terrorism and bombings that harass many cities of the world can be described as nothing but indications of madness.

## 2. Meditation Sickness and the Stress Complaint

There is no doubt that the modern world is filled with stress-causing elements. The situation is so widely recognized that, in the United States, employing a consulting lawyer and a psychoanalyst at the same time is considered a status symbol. But recently, among Americans who cannot afford a psychoanalyst, a strange way of working off stresses has become fashionable. It is called encounter group meditation.

A group of complete strangers comes together in a building and stands in a circle, holding hands, as if about to start a folk dance. As the circle moves, each person changes partners rhythmically. At each encounter, one person tells his partner his troubles (or anything he wants to say about himself); and the partner relates whatever he has on his own mind. The conversations become turbulent. Howls and rising dust accompany the groaning of the floor. The madness and mass hysteria that ensue are what is called transcendental meditation. In my opinion, however this transcendental meditation ought to be called the meditation sickness.

Another kind of sickness affects the Japanese at the present time. The English word *stress* has entered the Japanese language and now finds applications in all kinds of cases. As might be expected, problems associated with business conferences, commercial affairs, and management norms are considered stress causes. But stress is taken for an excuse in dealing with such things as tensions in personal relations, the commuter-traffic rush, crowds, or anything that has a deleterious effects on the mind or body. People make virtually pathological use of stress as a reason for getting out of whatever they do not want to do. In this sense, the Japanese suffer from what I call a stress complaint. Both the American meditation sickness and the Japanese stress complaint point to the large number of mentally disturbed people in modern society.

From the psychiatrist's standpoint, there are differences between these two sicknesses; but they share a common desire to escape from reality. This desire operates as a causative with special strength in the stress complaint and reveals the prevalence of the kind of fears that are symbolized by the three monkeys who are afraid to speak, hear, or see. Propelled by the desire to protect himself, the victim of the stress complaint foists off all responsibility on the stress factor. The meditation sickness is in effect an attempt to disperse tensions by giving boisterous expression to senses of inequality and frustration. In short, the individual tries to find stability by relying on the assistance of others. The stress complaint has deeper roots: self-pity, a sense of persecution, and the feeling of being the only person suffering from undue stress.

Although I suspect that the basis of the difference between the two is related to the differences between the American and the Japanese social structures, I am not qualified to speak as a specialist on the subject. The victim of the meditation sickness works out his problems by outwardly directed action; the stress-complaint sufferer turns inward and allows stress to accumulate.

# 3. The True Meaning of Meditation

I should now like to turn to a scientific, medical explanation of true meditation in constrast with encounter group meditation, or the meditation sickness. In his *Allgemeine Psychopathologie* (General Psychopathology), the German psychopathologist Karl Jaspers, the first person ever to devote attention to it in a medical connection, described meditation as discipline and said that mystics, sages, and saints in all major civilizations have followed such practices, to which he assigned various broad, deep contents. Jaspers claims that all kinds of meditation, no matter in what part of the world they are practiced, share a distinctive mental action: training for the sake of operation on consciousness in such a way as to work a relaxing change in it. The important point to note in this definition is the bold assertion that meditation itself is the thing that brings about the relaxing ·change in consciousness. In simpler terms, this concept explains meditation as self-control allowing a person to change his mental attitudes by means of his own strength. Jaspers further claimed that the basis of Johannes H. Schultz's autogenic training (self-hypnosis) was actual experience gained through meditation discipline. In addition, he insisted that seated Zen meditation has psychological therapeutic significance in that it is a way of training to alter consciousness, no matter whether one is or is not a believer in Zen Buddhism. The source of this therapeutic significance arises from the mental stability acquired as a result of the concentration of attention within the mind.

In this work, which appeared in 1950, Jaspers was the first person to direct attention toward oriental meditation as a discipline conducive to mental health. In spite of his rational, scientifically valid prophecy based on his intuition of the meaning of this kind of meditation, Jaspers lacked the technical skills to demonstrate scientific proof of his assertions. Or, perhaps, as he became more a philosopher and less a psychopathologist, he came to feel that the subject was no longer within the framework of his interests. Be that as it may, he deserves special notice for suggesting the possibility of scientific research in this field.

# 4. The Silent-enlightenment Experience

Jaspers saw that meditation discipline, apart from religious affiliation, includes scientifically valid elements, meaningful in psychological therapy. His realization that Zen meditation is universally valid because it deals with the point of juncture between the mental and physical is vitally important to psychiatry. Though there are many other aspects of meditation, perhaps the best order in which to deal with the subject is to begin with the scientific nature of seated Zen meditation. I started working on this issue quite by chance.

The bold, then still unproved hypothesis of Jaspers may have cast a shadow on my mind, where it lingered without my being fully aware. At any rate, one day, as I was walking through the Tokyo Kanda district, where there are many old book stores, my eye happened to fall on a work entitled *Mokushō Taiken no Kagaku* (Science of the silent-enlightenment experience), by Kanae Sakuma, a professor at the University of Tokyo. Thumbing through the book, I at once saw that the "silent enlightenment" was precisely the kind of stability—neither static nor dynamic—attained by means of the inner concentration achieved in meditation. The book was just what I had been looking for. As I walked and read with growing excitement, I learned that, though its religious aim is enlightenment, Doctor Sakuma insisted that, through the interior concentration it involves, seated Zen meditation can bring about scientifically verifiable mental and physical stability. The book was both a prophetic achievement and a suggestion for further study of the scientific nature of the results of attention concentration (engrossment). Doctor Sakuma said that scientific verification of the significance of seated Zen meditation could probably be found in the study of brain waves. He went on to suggest that not only the psychiatric, but also the actual functional cerebral changes produced by the silent-enlightenment experience could be studied by means of recently (about 1948) developed Western devices for measuring brain waves.

# 5. Zen and Meditation

In my efforts to justify the effects of meditation from the scientific standpoint, over the past fifteen years, I have measured the brain waves of about one hundred and fifty Zen Buddhist priests in more than a thousand interviews. Materials obtained in this way are carefully stored in my laboratory. Without the assistance and cooperation of these men, several of whom have already died, it might have been impossible for me to complete my work.

Buddhist philosophy explains all actions as the result of the harmonious interreaction of direct and indirect causes. Such causes were at work in bringing me together with these priests. And Buddhist compassion inspired them to cooperate so that religion and science could walk hand in hand for the benefit of both.

Seated Zen meditation is an inner concentration of attention performed to train the person to deepen his thoughts and cause them to bear meaningful fruit. The English word *meditation* is often used in translating the Japanese *Zazen* (seated Zen meditation) but it is not completely adequate because it underplays the element of training, which is of the utmost importance. Nor is intellectual concentration the same thing as seated Zen meditation. When the famous theoretical physicist Niels Bore was preparing his model of nuclear structure, he was obviously in a state of intellectual concentration, but this differs from the deepening of thought and emotions included in the concentration of attention attained in seated Zen meditation. Intellectual elements lie concealed in Zen meditation. In short, in states of this kind, the intellectual element is emphasized, and the training element virtually negated.

Karl Jaspers's use of the German word *die Versenkung* (concentration) is more accurate than *meditation*. But the important thing in this case is, as I have said, Jaspers's insistence that, divorced from their mystical and religious associations, such systems as Yoga and Zen meditation train people to concentrate for the sake of an altered state in consciousness.

I am in complete agreement: meditation without training bears no relation to seated Zen meditation. Furthermore, as Jaspers maintains, for Zen meditation to have effect, it must be conducted persistently and often. Only such training can result in a true fusion of mind and body. This is neither mystical nor intellectual. It is Zen meditation, in which the individual human being must engage in direct combat with himself.

Although in the preceding pages, I criticized what I call the encounter group meditation sickness, I do not reject it entirely. It too contains elements of training and, in a certain sense, overlaps with parts of the meditation employed in Zen discipline. The fault of the encounter-group system is that it forgets to adopt as a premise individual concentration of attention and deepening of thought. The goal of the encounter group is no more than mass rapture.

Zen meditative training is more isolated and private. Priests in Zen temples practice lonely seated meditation as a way of refining themselves. Oddly enough, foreigners often fail to understand this lonely aspect of such meditation and, upon visiting Japanese temples, complain that Zen has disappointed them. They feel that conflict and friction between the individual and his own self are uncomfortable. And so they are. But anyone who intends to compromise with the confrontation with himself will get nowhere with Zen meditation no matter how assiduously he tries. Sometimes people adopt the idea that Zen involves a cosmic awareness and an escape from the self. But this too is a facile and unproductive approach. Mistaken interpretations of this kind may be caused by initial teachers who follow the wrong philosophy.

Daisetz Suzuki, an undeniably great scholar, wrote many books in which he introduced Japanese Zen to the West. His achievements were great; but my own reconsiderations of the relations between seated Zen meditation and other kinds of meditation and my reflections on the evil of oriental mysticism that has surrounded Zen for a long time convince me that he had a strong and not entirely wholesome bias.

# 6. Significance of Zen Meditation for Today

Zen enjoys greater popularity in the West today and is not without followers in Japan. Its popularity may be explained on the basis of the healthful effects it has on the body. Nonetheless, the effects it has on the mind must not be overlooked. The attitudes of Westerners and Japanese toward their expectations of seated Zen meditation can be summarized as follows. In the West, people feel that Zen uncovers a true self that can help the everyday self overcome its present crises. They therefore strive to find the essence of the true self in Zen meditation. The Japanese take the practical approach of expecting Zen to help them solve their mental troubles. Both in the East and the West, people believe that Zen can bring them mental peace and tranquility. My own feeling is that the time has come for a modern reappraisal of Zen.

First, it would be a good idea for me to mention some of the preconceptions and dogmas that have come to be associated with Zen over many centuries. One of these is the doctrine that has arisen on the basis of ancient teachings to the effect that Zen does not rely on documents or other written works but on transmission of its philosophy directly from mind to mind. Another is the belief in a philosophy for discussion of Zen meditation that is built on a philosophical interpretation of human life and a living sense of values. Unfortunately, both of these doctrines continue unmitigated to the present and contribute to much confusion about Zen meditation.

The leading champion of the idea of a humanistic and value-oriented Zen meditation philosophy was Daisetz Suzuki, whose efforts have invited the mistaken impression that Zen is a brand of oriental mysticism. His English-language texts on the subject are logically composed and are understandable as attempts to explain the point of juncture between religion and philosophy. But, no matter how he tried to follow the general flow of Western rationalism, he seems to have been unable to steer clear of mysticism. Under his influence, Allan Watts wrote about Zen as something belonging to a remote and distant realm.

In their joint book, *Zen Buddhism and Psychoanalysis,* Suzuki and the psychoanalyst Erich Fromm wrote on the self, liberated from the frame of the self and thus enabled to find the true self. According to them, meditation frees the self from the realm of the unconscious. Through it, the self and the unconscious are sublimated into the cosmic unconscious. The authors do not elucidate the nature of the cosmic unconscious.

Their book is an attempt to explain a fusion between self-insight, the ultimate goal of psychoanalysis, and enlightenment, the ultimate goal of Zen Buddhism. But I do not think it succeeds. I might go so far as to say that it seems to be an attempt to embellish Zen and in some way to raise it to the level of a pseudoscience. The works is facile in its attempt to unify psychoanalysis and Zen on the basis of a mutual preunderstanding between Suzuki, who wanted to find the needed scientific substantiation for Zen in psychoanalysis, and Fromm, who hoped to find the ultimate goal of psychoanalysis in Zen. Regrettably, *Zen Buddhism and Psychoanalysis* distorts the truly scientific nature of Zen meditation and thereby hinders understanding. In the final analysis, it makes it seem that Zen and psychoanalysis are as incompatible as oil and water.

For a long time, people have taught—and some continue to teach—that Zen promises ease. This is surely a contradiction in terms. The disciplines of Zen are too demanding to be called easy. Nonetheless, there are those who insist that the human mind finds lasting comfort once it has mastered the techniques of Zen meditation. Perhaps this is the only interpretation of which the modern intellect is capable. Aldous Huxley claimed such elements for Zen, but I cannot believe that he understood the subject correctly.

I have discovered a discrepancy between Zen meditation as practiced by the Buddhist clergy and the practices advocated by such people as Daisetz Suzuki. At present there are two main streams of Zen, one represented by the Sōtō sect and the other by the Rinzai sect. Though both seek ultimate enlightenment, their approaches to their goal differ. Whereas Sōtō concentrates on Zen practices,

Rinzai spends much more time on the *kōan,* illogical question-and-answer problems that are thought to jolt the trainee to a higher state of understanding. Sōtō is more religious and Rinzai more philosophical in orientation.

The discrepancies between the way the two sects conduct seated Zen meditation make understanding difficult for foreigners and for the uninitiated Japanese. Many such people find their experiences with Zen disappointingly empty. To make matters worse, as long as the two major sects persevere in struggling to preserve mutually exclusive traditions, they will find it hard to teach Zen in a way that ordinary people can understand.

My own interpretation of the significance of Zen for our times is as outlined below. These impressions are, of course, intimately related with my research in brain waves.

It is said that, when he attained enlightenment under the pipal tree, Shakyamuni, the historical Buddha announced that all living beings possess the Buddha nature. In my opinion the best English word to use to describe that nature is *compassion.*

Clerical Zen teaches that the Buddha nature explained by Shakyamuni exists in all things—trees, stones, plants, animals, and all phenomena in the world of nature. According to this interpretation, the significance of meditation is trying to become one with all of the these; but I consider such an attempt at total unity contradictory. Shakyamuni became the Buddha, the Enlightened One, because he suffered in his attempts to find freedom from death, sickness, and the other sorrows of human life caused by exposure to threats from the world of nature. I do not think that the enlightenment experienced by Shakyamuni was the same as the compassion taught by the priesthood. He revealed the full Buddha nature innate in all human beings. Therefore, his enlightenment cannot have been a realization of his own Buddha nature since he had already shown that this is innate in all human beings. Instead, his enlightenment was the knowledge that escape from suffering is possible through meditation. The compassion he knew at that time was the desire to impart his knowledge to other suffering human beings.

A distorted interpretation of Shakyamuni's words leads to the paradoxical idea that enlightenment implies the possibility in all things in nature to attain compassion, or the Buddha nature. Further, it is a mistake and a delusion to interpret the Buddha nature as the ultimate goal of enlightenment. As I have already said, enlightenment was the realization that Shakyamuni attained through actual experience of the power of Zen meditation to free from suffering. Compassion, or the Buddha nature, is something entirely different, though Chinese Zen attempted to equate the two. Both the attempt and Chinese Zen itself failed because, in the face of actuality, the equation was impossible to make.

As I mentioned in the introduction, many Chinese monks fled to Japan at different historical times. They shared their knowledge with such local priests as Dōgen and Keizan, who, in their turn, earnestly sought to understand the true meaning of Zen meditation as practiced by Shakyamuni. For such men, meditation was not something philosophical or clerical, but a way of life leading to freedom from suffering. Though it was not their special property, the priests, realizing that Zen meditation has salutary effects on both mind and body and thus makes possible more successful training, did all they could to develop meditation practices. It was compassion that inspired them to want to help others to understand the merits of meditation. Shakyamuni, the Buddha, earned respect and became an object of religious veneration because he led others to such an understanding. His attitude is included in the practical training of Japanese Zen priests. It must be born in mind that Zen meditation is essentially practical. Of course, Zen is also Buddhism with both a religious and a philosophical nature.

As I have already said, Zen has a universality that includes and transcends both religion in general and Buddhism in particular and permeates the mind. The basic nature of that universality is Zen meditation itself, the key point of which is meditation training. Though my own experience with it is fairly brief and though I cannot be said to have attained enlightenment, I am convinced that fundamentally Zen training brings about an alteration in the consciousness. Zen meditation makes this especially clear. This further convinces me that enlightenment is a state reached by means of the kind of meditation or concentration that is called *samādhi* in Buddhist terminology.

Karl Jaspers pointed out that the psychological mechanism characteristic of such outstanding oriental meditation systems as Yoga and seated Zen meditation is an action performed deliberately by a person on his own consciousness to bring about an alteration in awareness. Further he said that this effect is one of practical fact observed from experience that must be divorced from matters of faith. In short, Jaspers showed that the condition achieved through training by the mystics, sages, and philosophers of the past is in fact a psychological state of mind and not a matter of religious faith or philosophy. This is the key to the universality of meditation, and failure to realize this has made it difficult to understand in the eyes of writers on the subject who have refused to regard it as a technique for bringing about an alteration in awareness.

Somewhat earlier than Jaspers, Kanae Sakuma carried out research on the psychological processes leading to Zen Buddhist enlightenment. His major research theme was *shikantaza*, or themeless meditation, practised by priests of the Sōtō Zen sect. He analyzed the contents of the thought of priests engaged in such meditation and discovered that a part of innate consciousness can be detonated by Zen meditation. The detonation of this part of consciousness he identified as enlightenment. Ordinarily, the human mind is moved to grief or joy by stimuli from the outside world. Zen meditation frees the mind from all superficial stimuli to allow it to reach what Sakuma termed basic consciousness. He made it clear that enlightenment is not a religious experience, but the attainment of insight by means of training that makes possible the manifestation in ordinary life of basic consciousness.

Of course, Zen Buddhism itself is a religion. But all people, whether believers in Zen or not, can employ the scientific aspects of the techniques of Zen meditation to bring about changes in their awareness and thus find mental stability and harmony. Furthermore, this can be done by the individual himself.

As is pointed out by an old Japanese proverb, egocentricity lies at the heart of the suffering of the world. This suffering and the egocentricity that cause it are part of human fate. Sigmund Freud posited a psychological structure in which the ego is the central axis of the personality. The id and the es operate from the world of instincts, and the superego controls the operations of the ego in the world of consciousness. The ego employs certain defense mechanisms to protect its territories from both the superego and the id and the es. Mental disorders result when these defense mechanisms break down. According to Freud, the defense mechanism is needed to protect the ego from something bad in the realm of the subconscious. The more practical Japanese approach represented in the proverb is that, no matter how he tries, a human being cannot escape suffering as long as he is alive since it is part of fate. This attitude is based on the belief that egocentricity and the desire for personal gain are fundamental to human desire. On the basis of such a belief, deliberate attempts to guide oneself lead, not to an elimination of suffering, but to its aggravation and increase.

Be that as it may, the goal of Zen Buddhism is emancipation from such suffering. I offer no objection to this goal, but I do insist that Zen meditation is not practiced for the sake of a direct release from suffering.

In the lives of busy members of modern society, egocentricity and the pursuit of personal gain are accepted as perfectly natural. Indeed, because the demand for intellectual production has become deeply rooted, egocentricity and the pursuit of gain might be termed the typical features of the consciousness of modern man; and values based on them are universally recognized. Since, without these two traits, people find it difficult to get along in the world, everyone today is to a greater or lesser extent intellectually polluted by them. Under such conditions, the enlightenment taught by Zen Buddhism is too remote to be meaningful. It is utopian rather than practical. Or it results in a Zen designed for the clergy but estranged from the ordinary people. Zen Buddhism does not show the way to salvation for modern man, since its only message is this: if you want enlightenment, practice seated Zen meditation. Without making any further growth, Zen is losing its former compassion, closing the door on itself, and becoming dereistic.

Though people today unconsciously demand an alteration of awareness that can guide them out of their dilemma, they do not show this need in the daily world of reality. Everyone suppresses or avoids questions about relations between the individual mind and the external environment. This may, indeed, be proof of the efficient operation of human mental defense mechanisms. People who follow such a policy are successful in pursuit of personal gain. They have no connection with Zen meditation because they are entirely adapted to the outside world and the affairs of everyday life. Perhaps they have become people without ego structures. I am by no means despising such people.

Thought its nature is difficult to pin down precisely, suffering undeniably exists in the minds of countless people today. Many people who feel the need of an alteration of consciousness seek it in the defense mechanism of psychological analysis, which becomes in itself a kind of defense mechanism. This enables them to adapt to daily life. But people devoted to this practice can hope for no success in Zen meditation without a change of viewpoint.

The psychiatrist realizes a deep anxiety in even such people. Their insecurities assume the forms of neuroses and such psychopathological symptoms as nervous gastritis and other disorders, which are on the increase. What these people actually need is not adaptation, but adjustment.

By adjustment, I mean the state of mind in which the person can cooperate with the outside world and with other people without sacrificing self-esteem. But maintaining such a frame of mind is difficult now and will probably become more difficult in the future.

The major effect of Zen meditation is the way in which it enables the individual to preserve self-esteem, strengthen himself, and develop an attitude that helps him to live in harmony with others. I shall explain the scientific reasons for this later. But at this point, I should like to call attention to a comment made by Keizan, one of the founders of Japanese Zen, who, in his *Zazen Yōjinki* (The Essential Method of Seated Zen Meditation), described Zen meditation as very much like relaxing at home. In other words, he recommended that one should leave behind the clamor of the world of affairs and attempt to examine the heart of things in the kind or relaxed meditation possible only in the calm of the home.

I am neither denying nor rejecting enlightenment as the goal of Zen Buddhist research, nor am I ignoring the importance of salvation from the suffering of the world. I do, however, express doubts about Zen meditation that has Zen enlightenment as its goal. Not everyone is in a position to become a Zen monk. Furthermore, I suspect religious delusions in the claims of all Zen monks who insist that they have reached enlightenment as an outcome of enthusiastic Zen meditation.

The significance of Zen meditation lies in the way in which it shows that no amount of adaptability and self-defense mechanism will enable people living in the secular world to surpass their own egoism and greed for gain. Seated Zen meditation teaches that this impossibility is not contradictory, but good because it is a part of the general plan of things.

Relying on Zen meditation for enlightenment is a matter for the Buddhist clergy. Perhaps it is a deluded attempt to convert an intellectual operation into such meditation. I do not believe that Zen meditation alone can lead to an enlightened condition. Under no religious faith or tenet can enlightenment, once achieved, be universal. These are my reasons for saying that Zen meditation cannot always lead to enlightenment.

Enlightenment is personal and can be many things to many different people. The state that Henry David Thoreau experienced as a result of his more than two years by Walden Pond can be called enlightenment, as can the rejection of reality of the Hippies. Professor Kouji Satō has described the ecstatic state experienced by people who use the alcaloide compound known as $LSD_{25}$ as identical to Zen enlightenment. If this is true, the formula Hippy life $+ LSD_{25}$ could equal a shortcut to the ultimate goal of Zen.

As I have already mentioned, in Rinzai Zen, trainees are given problems called *kōan* to solve. If their answers are satisfactory, they are advanced in training ranks and, as a token, are given new titles. A certain trainee was once enlightened to this knowledge: "I am the center; I am the universe; I am the creator."

In short, enlightenment finds highly individual expression. But it was described by Erich Fromm and Daisetz Suzuki, in their *Zen Buddhism and Psychoanalysis* in this way: "If we would try to express enlightenment in psychological terms, I would say that it is a state in which the person is completely turned to the reality outside and inside of him, a state in which he is fully aware of it and grasps it. *He* is aware of it—that is, not his brain, nor any other part of his organism, but *he*, the whole man. He is aware of it; not as an object over there which he grasps with his thought, but *it*, the flower, the dog, the man, in its or his full reality. He who awakens is open and responsive to the world, and he can be open and responsive because he has given up holding on to himself as a thing, and thus has become empty and ready to receive. To be enlightened means 'the full awakening of the total personality to reality.'"

Though there may be arguments as to the absolute value of this book as a whole, the emphasis on being aware in the comment of Fromm and Suzuki sets their interpretation apart from the alteration of awareness of Jaspers; Sakuma's interpretation of Zen meditation; and the states attained by means of Yoga, transcendental meditation, and other methods. In Zen meditation, the awareness by the individual of an awakening is the important thing. I believe that the process of Zen meditation is a training method including enlightenment. And this is its significance for modern times. It is the ability to make people aware that gives Zen its universality apart from religious faith and doctrine. I have discovered a new scientific nature in Zen meditation. And it is now possible to explain the relation between Zen and the mind in scientifically convincing terms. This possibility came about with the uncovering of the universal and scientific aspects of the actual practice of Zen meditation.

# Seated Meditation

## 1. Briefly about Brain Waves

Before delving more deeply into the way this knowledge is helpful in the scientific application of Zen meditation, I should like to explain briefly the kinds of waves emitted by the brain and the psychological states they indicate.

Many years of study of the brain waves, the only indicator we have of the condition of the brain, have shown the following things. When the brain is in a state of relaxed calm, it emits waves called alpha waves. But when it is in a state of tension it emits either beta waves or the still more intense gamma waves. In all states of

FIG. 1   Changes in mental state affect the kind of brain waves emitted.

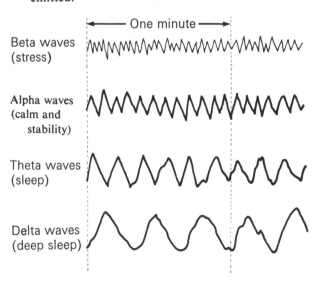

complete rest and repose—except the unconsciousness caused by attacks of epilepsy—the brain emits theta or delta waves (see FIG. 1). In short, when a person is angry, irritated, or upset, his brain emits beta waves; when his anger reaches fighting intensity, his brain begins to emit gamma waves. During periods of prolonged tension, beta waves predominate, and almost no alpha waves appear. If, however, a way were devised to cause it to emit only alpha waves, the brain would remain free of tension.

## 2. Posture Regulation

### (1) Zen Meditation in Sitting Posture

This chapter deals with the Zen principle that the posture of the body affects the mind and attempts to examine the positions used for Zen meditation and to explain their effects and the best ways to take advantages of them. The influence of posture on mental attitudes is apparent in many aspects of daily life. When we are about to come into contact with some great danger, we stand up straight. When we have something important to say, we sit straight in our chairs. Healthy and cheerful people more often stand with chest out and shoulders back than with back bent. The ancient oriental codes of courtesy and martial arts invariably begin by teaching proper posture. But it is Zen that has taught the relation between the posture (and breathing) and the condition of the mind. In the writings of such great priests as Dōgen there are passages explaining that the mind and the body are one and that each influences the other. To regulate the mind, it is necessary to regulate the body—the breathing and the posture. In this way it is possible to store up physical energy and unite it with mental energy.

Of course, other schools of philosophy and religion have insisted on the oneness of mind and body. Jean-Paul Sartre and Martin Heidegger among the Existentialists are only two of the noted advocates of the basic concept that the body and the mind cannot be separated. The psychoanalyst Wilhelm Reich interprets human beings in terms of organic processes and attempts to find common energies and factors underlying both the mind and the body. He describes as chronic muscle contraction such conditions as stiff neck and chin, unusually full chest or breast, and tightly pinched waists and says that they are characteristic of people who are mentally constricted and unable to express themselves freely. Physiology of the brain offers adequate substantiation of the idea of the unity of the mind and the body. The cerebral cortex controls consciousness; and the central autonomic nervous system controls the unconsciously regulated functions of the body, which sustain life. These two important organs operate in opposition; that is, when the cerebral cortex is stimulated to great activity, the central autonomic nervous system is repressed and vice versa. Brain-wave patterns and observations of breathing and pulse rate prove that this is true, but I should like to go into the theoretical reasons for the phenomenon in somewhat greater detail.

Many people have experienced first stomach disorders and then actual pain as a consequence of emotional or psychological stress that has lasted for several days. Zen meditation can prevent this kind of situation. The reason for this is related to the effect such meditation has on the autonomic nervous system, irregularity and dullness in which cause stomach disorders and pain. Zen meditation regulates the operation of the autonomic system and relaxes tensions that affect the cerebral cortex. In this way it brings stability to the spirit and returns health to the body. In other words, by maintaining balance between the operations of the cerebral cortex and the central autonomic nervous system, it helps create a smooth, well-ordered state of mind. This is the scientific corroboration for the Zen teaching that the mind and the body are one.

Operating on the belief that the movement of the body itself reflects the stability of the mental state of the person, we performed an experiment involving nine Zen priests highly experienced in seated meditation and nine people ranging in age from twenty-five

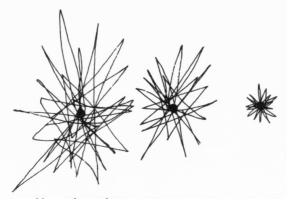

Neurotic patient   Ordinary person   Zen priest

FIG. 2   The lines leading outward from the central dot indicate body movements.

to sixty-two who were totally without experience in this kind of
mental and physical discipline. We had these people go through
thirty minutes of Zen meditation in any of several positions. Using
a device involving a suspended lead weight with an inked tip and
white drawing paper, we recorded the amounts and directions of
sway in the upper body of each meditating person. Reconstructions
of averages taken from the actual recorded charts are shown in
FIG. 2. No matter what position the people assumed, the bodies
of the experienced Zen priests moved much less and much less
erratically than those of the inexperienced people. Later we
plotted charts of the body movement of people simply sitting and
relaxing without any thought of Zen meditation. The results of
these tests showed that body movement in such people under such
circumstances is frequent and extensive. We then felt that we had
come close to showing that mental and physical stability are
intimately related, but we decided to make another test to sub-
stantiate this theory further.

We conducted the same body movement test on nine patients
known to be suffering from neuroses; the experiment took place
in the same room as the one conducted on the priests and the
inexperienced Zen meditators and lasted for the same amount

of time: thirty minutes. The results were startling. As can be seen from the reconstructed average movement patterns of these patients, the movements of the body of a person suffering extreme mental instability are more erratic and wider than those of a normal person without Zen-meditation experience. In short, the mentally stable person can remain physically stable for a fixed period of time. The smaller the range of his body movement in that period of time, the more stable his mind is likely to be.

But now I must turn to the question of posture that is of great importance in Zen meditation. The two major reasons for controlling the body position in meditation are to correct posture and improve the functioning of the internal organs, particularly, the stomach and the intestines. Though these purposes are listed separately here, they are in fact inseparable.

The teachings of Zen argue that there is no difference between the active and the static conditions and that the two are one. This is the meaning of the Zen-meditation posture. Though the meditator strives for complete immobility, he must not sleep. On the contrary, though he appears static, he is actually filled with abundant vitality. In short, though not moving, he is in a dynamically active state, as can be proved by records of his brain waves. I shall deal with this problem in detail later, but for the present, it is important to remember that the Zen body-control method is intended to develop calm with action and action with calm. This is true no matter whether the person is sitting perfectly still or is engaged in violent physical action. But what is the best posture to assume in order to maintain calm in action and action in calm?

First of all, the position one assumes must be stable. Second, it must cause very little discomfort and no bodily strain since to develop the bodily and mental controls that are the major aim of Zen meditation requires that one hold this position for from fifteen to twenty minutes. On the other hand, the position must stimulate sufficient tension to enable one to concentrate. A very comfortable position is fine for sleeping, but not very good for Zen meditation. Over many years, the masters of Zen have devised positions that meet these three standards—stability, relative comfort and tension—exactly.

Modern medical science has proved that, though they may have been unaware of it, in devising the meditation postures, the priests of old developed positions that are excellent in that they do not apply undue pressure on the vertebrae and therefore do not constrict or dull the autonomous nerves in the vicinity of the vertebrae. I shall now discuss the three positions used in the Zen body-control system: sitting, standing, and lying down.

Seated Zen meditation begins with the assumption of a position based on the one the Buddha is thought to have assumed when he sat meditating under the pipal tree. Priests of course wear clerical garments when meditating, but ordinary people may wear their customary clothes. It is important to loosen all belts and other binding items of clothing and to remove wristwatches or anything else that might prove distracting. It is unnecessary to remove eyeglasses.

Next place a thick cushion on the floor and sit so that about half of your buttocks rest on it. Zen priests use a special round, thick cushion called a *zafu*, which symbolizes membership in the clergy. But any ordinary cushion is suitable as long as it is of moderate thickness and hardness.

You must be barefooted. Place the left foot, sole upward, on the right thigh and the right foot, again sole up, on the left thigh. At first this position seems difficult; but, with adjustments in the position of the cushion and with time, you will become accustomed to it. It is called the *kekka-fuza*, or full-crossed-legs position.

Depending on bodily build, this position may be difficult to assume. For instance, people with long legs find it very uncomfortable. In such cases, assume the *hanka-fuza* or semi-crossed-legs position. In this position, the foot of one leg only is put on the opposite thigh. The remaining foot is put under the opposite thigh. Adjust even this position if necessary; the important thing is to get into a position that feels confortable (Fig. 3).

Place your hands at a point between your legs. The right hand, palm up, must be on the bottom and the left hand, palm up, on the top. The two thumbs are bent, and their first joints are brought lightly together (FIG. 4). Putting your hands in this position automatically causes your elbows to part from the sides of your body and your shoulders to relax. At the same time, it causes

FIG. 3 The two seated positions for Zen meditation: full-crossed-legs position (left) and semi-crossed-legs position (right). The cushion is called a *zafu*.

FIG. 4 Positions for the hands in seated Zen meditation. The hands are palms up, the left resting in the right and the thumbs touching lightly. Ideally, the tip of the right middle fingers should fall at about the second joint of the left middle finger.

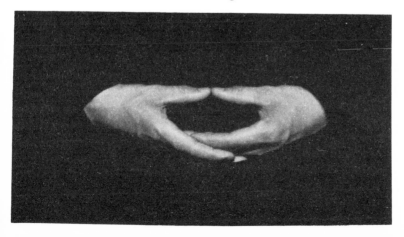

Fig. 5 It is important that the eyes remain open during seated Zen meditation. The lips and mouth will relax naturally if the tip of the tongue is placed lightly against the upper teeth. If this is done and if the hands are held as shown in Fig. 4, the position shown above will be maintained.

you to straighten your spine and to hold the topmost part of your head in a line perpendicular to the earth. Your face will be turned slightly downward to the front and the rear two-thirds of your head will be in line with a perpendicular to the earth. The tip of your tongue should barely touch the backs of your front teeth. This will cause you to close your mouth in such a way that your lips touch lightly (Fig. 5).

When you are in this position, your kneecaps and your backbone delineate a right triangle, on the apex (the point beneath your spine) of which rests the weight of your trunk. A person who has mastered it can sit in this position for a long time without fatigue and without numbness in the body or legs.

Your gaze must fall at a spot about one meter in front of you. During meditation, your eyes remain naturally open and fixed at a point in space (FIG. 6). I shall explain later why it is important that your eyes should remain open during meditation. The longer a person has been engaging in Zen meditation, the better his meditating position—no matter whether it is the full-crossed-legs or the semi-crossed-legs position. Mastering this position—I call it regulating the body—is the first step in Zen meditation. The

FIG. 6   The ideal seated-Zen-meditation position seen from a position diagonally to the side. The entire body is relaxed, and the head is lowered slightly forward. The eyes are open.

FIG. 7   A mature Zen priest in the seated meditation position,
seen from the front.

photograph in FIG. 7 shows experienced Zen priests in the meditation position.

For the sake of beginners, I should like to add a few more ex-
planatory remarks. Although, once the person has become
accustomed to regular Zen meditation, it makes no difference
where it is performed, at the start, it is wise to choose a quiet place.
Always carry out the meditation exercise at the same time each
day. In this way, Zen meditation will become a part of everyday

life; and you will find that persevering in it is easier. It is a good idea to meditate in the morning immediately upon awaking or in the evening just before going to bed. At first, five or ten minutes is long enough, but the meditation sessions ought to be increased gradually to from twenty to thirty minutes. The following points too are of importance. Do not attempt to meditate when you have had insufficient sleep or are overtired. Do not meditate immediately after meals or when you are very hungry. Dress lightly but stay warm. Before meditating, refresh yourself by washing your hands and face.

The *kekkaf-uza* and the *hanka-fuza* are the standard seated meditation positions, but it is also possible to meditate seated in a chair. In such a case, the knees are spread; and the heels are together. This position too creates a triangle—either equilateral or isosceles—on which the weight of the upper body can rest.

Before going on to the other two major categories of Zen meditation positions, I should like to explain how the principles of seated meditation can be applied to daily-life situations to help you have a clearer head and greater concentration when you must attend meetings or conferences or face situations in which lucidity and attention are of paramount importance. The method I prescribe is very simple: assume the relaxed seated position. Three hand positions are satisfactory: folded and placed over the navel, palms down on each knee, or on each thigh with fingers spread and palms down. Of the three, the last is best because it causes the shoulders to relax and to fall into a natural position. Seated in this position, the body is in a state of calm in action and action in calm. It is possible to give complete attention to each word the other person is saying and to be ready to react promptly and to give concise, direct answers to all questions as long as suitable balance between relaxation and tension is maintained.

From personal experience I can say that this position enables one to act with alertness and accuracy even when sleepy from a long night of study or perhaps poker. Indeed, I think this position proves so helpful in daily affairs, that I shall enumerate the steps involved in assuming it in list form.

1. Sit well back in the chair.
2. Spread your legs comfortably; your thighs will form an angle of from thirty to ninety degrees.
3. Bring your heels together and spread your feet to form an angle of about ninety degrees.
4. Rest your hands, palms down, lightly on your thighs. The palms of the hands should not come in contact with the thighs.

As in the other seated positions, the relaxed seated posture unifies the spirit by regulating the body and helps the brain to function better.

### (2) Meditation in a Reclining Posture

As has already been said, the reclining posture is one of the positions in which Zen meditation is possible. Some years ago, when I and my colleagues at Tokyo University were conducting brain-wave tests on a group of Zen priests in a temple in Tokyo, it became necessary for us to live, eat, and sleep at the temple for a limited period. During that time, I observed the curious fact that all of the priests slept on their sides. In ordinary circumstances, when a person is resting after a day's work, he lies flat on his back. Was it possible that even in sleep the Zen priests did not rest? To answer this question I discussed the matter with some of the priests and learned the following. Sleeping as well as waking, these men conduct Zen disciplines; and while asleep they must make use of the general principles of the seated meditation position. I have called this kind of meditation, sleeping Zen.

Interestingly, in recent years, the Belgian neurophysiologist E. Bremer, the Americans W. Magoun and R. French, and the Japanese Toshihiko Tokizane have shown that in physiological terms the human brain is designed to function when the body is reclining. Sleeping Zen, which makes use of this innate characteristic of the brain in a discipline continued during slumber, is not limited to priests who have made special studies of the topic. Anyone can practice sleeping Zen.

The posture adopted for sleep by Zen priests is very much like the one seen in representations of the entry of the Buddha into Nirvana. The Buddha is lying on his side with his head pillowed on one arm. Physiologically, this position is good for the body. Seen from the front or the back, the vertebrae are virtually straight, with only a slight S-curve deviation to right and left. Seen from the lateral view, however, the vertebrae swell forward in a pronounced curve at the chest and back in again in a curve in the hip region. Lying on the side, therefore, puts much less stress on the vertebrae and the nerves of the spinal chord than lying on the back. Zen priests sleep in this position. In the winter they use only a thin pallet-style mattress; in the summer they sleep on a still thinner mat of straw. This rigid discipline is too severe for the beginner in Zen meditation. Nor is there any need to change from a comfortable bed to a hard pallet. Sleeping Zen can be performed with whatever bedding you are accustomed to using, but the following experiment conducted on Zen priests will show the kind of effect their system can have.

Measurement of the brain waves of sleeping ordinary people has shown that most of us follow a regular pattern. At first, when the person becomes drowsy, the brain emits stable alpha waves. As sleep gains the upper hand, the brain stops emitting these and begins emitting low-cycle theta waves, characteristic of sleep. Gradually, these give way to still lower-cycle delta waves, characteristic of deep sleep. At first, when a bystander calls out to the sleeper, the brain will respond by emitting higher-cycle waves. The procedure by which this is accomplished is called the K complex of waves. Gradually, however, sleep deepens still further; and the brain gives off a preponderance of very low-cycle waves. When this state is reached, noises and slight shakings fail to arouse response.

Measurements of the brain waves of sleeping Zen priests produce the same results with one important difference. No matter how deep the priest's sleep, he is always ready to respond to outside stimuli. This is true even when the brain is emitting only very low-cycle waves. Of course, the daily discipline of the Zen priesthood to an extent accounts for this ability, but the importance of the sleeping position—on the side—must not be overlooked.

Earlier I said that sleeping Zen consists in sleeping on one's side and that there is no need to change from a comfortable bed to the pallets of Zen priests. This is true because, when placed on the side, the body forms an almost completely horizontal line from head to feet, with a slight S-curve in the spine. This means that the perfectly horizontal posture is natural for the body in this position, no matter what kind of material it is resting on. Consequently, traveling and having to sleep on strange beds, two of the frequently mentioned causes of occasional insomnia, do not affect a person who rests in the sleeping Zen position. Furthermore, the habitual insomniac can find relief from his complaint by adopting this sleeping position. Indeed, people who come to the Tokyo University Hospital complaining of insomnia in light to moderate stages of intensity may be cured by no more than a change to this position.

Sleeping in this natural position, which puts no pressures on the spinal chord, promotes the health and vigorous functioning of the autonomic nervous system, which controls the heart, lungs, stomach, intestines, and other internal organs. This means that sleeping Zen can contribute to the cure of chills, high-blood pressure, constipation, diarrhea, loss of appetite and other similar minor, but distressing, conditions. The way it can bring about a cure of the chills of hands and feet of women—especially middle-aged women—who suffer in winter or whenever the temperature drops sharply is only one illustration of my meaning.

These chills of the hands and feet are caused by constriction of the capillaries. The autonomic nervous system controls the functioning and the health of the capillaries; therefore, when a natural sleeping position is adopted to stimulate the more vigorous functioning of that system, the capillaries perform their roles more effectively, and chills cease.

### (3) Standing Posture

Standing is clearly a more active mode than the sitting and reclining postures that have been the subject of the preceding discussions.

Indeed there may be some people among my readers who doubt that bodily control of this kind is applicable to the standing position. Yet in modern life, we all stand—and suffer from prolonged standing—to such an extent that anyone would welcome a way to make positive use of this posture in a kind of bodily control that transforms the pain of standing into profit. For example, who would not be happy to know a body-control method that makes use of the time wasted waiting for the bus or for a date who is habitually late?

The way a person stands reveals much about his mental and physical condition. The man who is waiting in line to buy a ticket for the next race at the race track manifests his impatience by shifting from foot to foot and fidgeting. The person who feels unwell leans on something or bends forward. The member of the national assembly who disagrees with the motion being passed leaps to his feet, cranes his neck, and waves his arms angrily until the president of the organization recognizes him. Emotional and physical stability too find expression in a stable standing position.

My way of developing bodily stability in the standing position, which enables you to remain on your feet without tiring for long periods, involves two points: plane equilibrium and the ability to use the flexibility of your knees to counter any movement that might occur in the plane on which you are standing. It is essential to develop a consciousness of this plane and to be constantly aware that it might tremble or tilt. Standing is the best way to cultivate this awareness; when one is seated on an aircraft or train, one is much less conscious of the plane on which one rests than when one stands. Once you are aware of the plane and are prepared for its motion, when it does tilt or tremble, you can adjust the positions of your legs and your vertebrae to ensure that your body weight falls on a line that is always perpendicular to the plane. For instance, if you are on a vehicle, bend the right or left knee as is required by its motion. No matter how crowded the vehicle, no matter how the people around you may lean or fall, you will remain stable because your body will maintain the correct relation with the plane on which it rests. And this is the key to stability in all standing positions. Correct relation to the plane on which the body stands and the ability to be able to conform to possible changes in it enable the famous guards at Buckingham Palace to stand for hours without tiring or flinching.

Now I shall explain how to cultivate this sense in somewhat more concrete terms. Think of your legs as springs and of the soles of your feet as being made of sponge. Your arms should hang relaxed at your sides like the weights of an old-fashioned wall clock. Your fingers should barely graze the sides of your thighs. As a natural result of this position, your shoulders will assume a comfortable position, and your head and neck will remain stable and unaffected by the contractions of your knees. Your gaze should fall about two meters in front of you. Thinking of your legs as springs may give you some difficulty, but the technique can be mastered if you follow these simple steps. Bend your knees slightly to relax them. Spread your legs slightly apart; thrust your hips slightly forward and downward. This will allow your legs to act as springs which can be balanced by the slight movement of your arms, which, as I have said, must be hanging at your sides like the weights of a clock. The lightness and flexibility of stance that you will develop if you follow these directions will give you balance in moving vehicles and will allow you to remain on your feet untired for long times. It is interesting that this same kind of stance is used in many of the Japanese martial arts including kendo fencing and judo.

Patients of melancholia often develop distressing symptoms because they lose the awareness of the plane on which they stand and consequently fail to make the effort to keep their bodies perpendicular to that plane. I recall a patient suffering from this condition who told me that going to work in the morning was terrifying because the pavements and halls he had to travel seemed to be twisting and slanting. The walkways seemed to pitch, and his own feet seemed to float instead of treading firmly on the ground. But later this man came to realize what I meant by being prepared to conform to the movement of the plane on which he stands. Furthermore, he was able to apply this purely physical advice to the world of emotions and to see that flexibility is needed to face the unforeseeable changes that take place in daily life. When he saw that my advice was true, he began to recover from the depression that had plagued him.

The same standing body stability method once helped a patient of mine overcome severe motion sickness from which she had suffered from childhood. Her condition was so bad that she was forced to forgo the pleasure of a honeymoon trip because she knew she would become ill and vomit if she rode a vehicle, no matter what it was. I taught her the basics of stability in standing— awareness of the plane and preparedness to conform to motion— and measured her brain waves, respiration, and pulse. Some while later, upon receiving a telegram from her mother to the effect that her father had fallen ill, she resolved to return to her rural home by train, even if it might mean motion sickness. When she returned to Tokyo after her father's recovery, she called on me to explain delightedly that the standing-body-stability system had enabled her to ride all the way home on a train without the slightest discomfort. And this marked the end of her long suffering from motion sickness. At the time of this visit, I once again measured her brain waves, pulse, and respiration to find that they were all much more steady than they had been on the earlier occasion.

# 3. Breath Regulation

## (1) Reducing Breath Frequency

Modern man lives under permanent stress. Upon waking he dashes from bed to get ready for work. He must hurry to catch the train or drive along crowded highways to reach his office. Throughout the day he is under the strain of helping his own company keep up with or surpass its competitors while trying to see to it that he is not overtaken by any of his fellow workers. Often he must do overtime work until the late hours of the night and then plod a weary way home only to face the alarm clock and the same routine the following morning. Both the pace and the severe competition of life in the modern city act constantly and detrimentally on the nerves of the average person. Heart specialists say that the rate of deaths of heart disease is especially high among the middle level of administrative personnel and white-collar workers. In a society subject to inflation, environmental pollution, excess traffic, and newspapers filled with nothing but gloom, all of us face strains and tensions that are enough to do permanent damage to heart and mind alike. Nor is the tension limited to adults. Children as well face serious stress-causing situations in school every day.

Of course, the heart and the nerves require suitable stimulus and moderate tension to function and develop, but excess tension and stimulus can make a mental and physical wreck of an individual. Modern man is subject to tensions and stresses of excess intensity, and unless he finds a way to divert himself from these strains he is likely to collapse. Many of the patients in mental hospitals are disturbed primarily because they cannot devise diversions for themselves.

Sometimes, these people try to face tensions directly and force themselves to do something to relax, but this rarely has an effect. The only way to defeat tension is to apply guerrilla tactics. Do not approach the enemy head-on; instead, attack him from the flank. In other words, counter a stress-causing stimulus by applying another stimulus from another direction. This stimulus can take the form of a friendly drink on the way home or a game of cards with office companions. Anything of this kind can relax the tensions of the daily grind, as office workers in all parts of the world are usually quick to discover.

But these diversions are only temporary and if indulged in to excess can do more harm than good. The kind of relief from stress that I shall explain next is one that contributes to the increase of health and well-being and that requires no special place and no additional people to perform. The relief I prescribe comes from breath control.

In Zen temples, breath control is taught first to beginners and novice priests. When the position of the body is correct and when the breathing has been regulated, the mind enters the calm state in which profound meditation is possible. I have performed experiments on the brain waves of meditating Zen priests that prove this to be true. For example, priests insist that when worldly thoughts interfere with their meditation, they may return their minds to the proper state by correcting their posture and regulating their breathing. I once measured the brain waves of a meditating priest. At one point, the calm, steady flow of alpha waves stopped to be replaced by an outflow of beta waves, indicating emotional and mental tension. Before long, the priest corrected his breathing; and, in a short time, the beta waves stopped, and the alpha waves reappeared. When the meditation session was over, I questioned the priest, who told me that at the time when I observed the change from alpha to beta waves, he had been distracted and that after he regained control of his breathing he once again entered profound meditation. It was at this time that the beta waves gave way to a reappearance of alpha waves.

That this ancient breathing control system has salutary effects on body and mind alike is proved by the use to which it is put in modern treatment of psychiatric patients. In this chapter I shall examine the several ways to control the breath and shall relate them to daily life and to scientific research. I recommend that you include one or many of them in your daily living. The first method is reducing breath frequency.

Under ordinary conditions, the human being breathes about eighteen times a minute. This frequency increases when the person engages in strenuous activity. The priest in Zen meditation, however, breathes only four or five times each minute. Prolonging exhalation is one way to reduce the number of breaths. Zen teachings say that one should exhale very slowly and so gently that the flow of air would not disturb a feather attached to the tip of the nose. At the end of exhalation, air will be inhaled quickly into the lungs. Exhale slowly through the nose and inhale naturally through the nose. This breathing method involves the abdominal as well as the thoracic muscles. You should practice doing this until you breathe only four or five times a minute.

This is difficult to do at first, but the following system will help the beginner reduce his respiratory rate to ten breaths a minute. When he reaches this stage, he need only continue to train to reduce it still further.

First, memorize the numbers one to ten in Japanese: one—*hitotsu*, two—*futatsu*, three—*mittsu*, four—*yottsu*, five—*itsutsu*, six—*muttsu*, seven—*nanatsu*, eight—*yattsu*, nint—*kokonotsu*, ten —*tō*. At the beginning of the first exhalation, say slowly *hi-to-tsu*. When you get to *tsu*, exhale. Continue this all the way to *tō*, which you must extend to *to-ho-o*, and you will have breathed ten times.

One good place to practice breath control is on crowded commuter trains. Many people with jobs in cities must ride for hours every day to reach their places of work. If you are one of them, you can put this time to good use by doing breath-control exercises that require no special postures and that are not disturbing to people around you. No matter how much the train reels and no matter how your neighbor may crowd you, simply close your eyes to block out possible distractions and inhale quickly and exhale as slowly as possible. Not only will this help you to prepare yourself to be calm to face whatever the day may hold, it will also contribute to better health if you do it every day. Many old people in Japan attribute their continued vigor to breath control and reduction of breathing frequency. Furthermore, breath control of this kind is the foundation of all the other breath-control systems and of mental and physical health systems in general.

But let us examine the physiology of breathing in an attempt to see why slow breathing is more efficient. As is obvious, breathing is divided into two stages each of which performs a special function. Inhalation carries a fresh supply of oxygen to the lungs. Exhalation removes from the body the carbon dioxide that is taken from the blood and stored in the lungs until it can be expelled. Unlike the operations of the heart and other internal organs, breathing is partly subject to conscious control. For instance, women who dive for abalone and other shellfish in Japan train to hold their breath for a long time in order to remain underwater as long as possible. Breathing is not, however, entirely consciously controlled. Breath automatically resumes when it has been held for a dangerous length of time. Furthermore, during sleep, breathing is completely automatic. Indeed, throughout much of our waking time as well we breathe without being aware of it. The rate of breathing automatically changes in accordance with the body's needs. The autonomic nervous system mediates this function. When a person has indulged in some sudden or violent activity that demands great energy output, the breathing rate increases.

It is unknown exactly how many times a minute the human being ought to breathe. The eighteen breaths a minute that are the average for people in relaxed state is not necessary to life. But it is certain that the idea that rapid breathing affords the body a richer supply of oxygen is mistaken. Indeed, because it is shallow, rapid breathing fails to carry the needed oxygen to the lungs but allows it to escape in the bronchial tubes. Moreover, it fails to remove all carbon dioxide and in this way reduces the amount of space in the lungs available to a supply of fresh oxygen. But if you exhale slowly and completely so that no carbon dioxide remains, a pressure differential will develop, and air will naturally rush in to fill the now empty lungs. Since much more oxygen is taken to the lungs with this kind of breathing, using it, one can comfortably reduce the breath rate to four or five breaths a minute.

As the middle-aged man who finds his heart pounding and his breathing rapid and irregular after climbing the same number of flights of steps that in youth he bounded up with no ill effects knows, short breath is not a sign of good physical condition. Nor is it indicative of mental composure, since short breath accompanies fright, neurosis, and some more serious disturbances.

In the first place, slow deep breathing lightens the load the heart must bear. As is well known, the heart pumps to all parts of the body the blood that carries oxygen taken in by the lungs. When breathing is fast, as it often is after physical exertion, the breathing rate increases; and the heart must beat faster to carry out its function. This means that under rapid breathing conditions, the heart must work harder than usual. On the other hand, when breathing is deep and slow, the heart can do its work with less effort. But, in order to understand this better, one must know a little more about the functions of the heart itself.

The heart is controlled by the autonomic nervous system, composed of the sympathetic and the parasympathetic nerves, which work in opposition to each other. When the sympathetic nerves are excited, the heart beats more rapidly; and the pulse rate increases. The parasympathetic nerves have the opposite effect of slowing the heartbeat and the pulse rate. As long as balance is maintained between the operations of the two sets of nerves, no problems arise. But when the sympathetic nerves, in response to some kind of abnormal stress, remain in a state of excitement, they keep the heart working overtime and in this way increase the load it must bear. No matter how much we should like to be able to cause the heart to slow down when it is overworked, we cannot since it is controlled by the autonomic nervous system, which is not subject to conscious control.

Still, breath control has a pronounced effect on the operation of the heart. For example, Yoga breath-control exercises are said to bring the heart to a complete halt. In fact, however, this is only a great reduction in blood pressure and a lightening of the operation of the heart caused by very slow breathing. This effect can only be achieved by highly experienced Yogis. I mention it here because it reveals the kind of effect breath control can have and should show the reader how valuable he can make his commuting time by practicing breathing exercises on the train or bus. Neurotic people sometimes complain that, when afraid of being late, after punching their time card at the door and arriving at their desk, they are in a state of upset characterized by rapid, difficult breathing and increased pulse rate. No doubt they have allowed themselves to create this condition on the way to work. How much better their time would have been spent if they had used it to slow their breathing and calm themselves.

The effect of reduced breathing rate is by no means limited to the body, but extends to the mind and the emotions as well. It is true that slow, calm breathing brings composure and a natural relaxation of emotional sufferings. By controlling and regulating the breath completely, one obtains control over one's entire self and therefore remains mentally calm in the face of emotional disturbances. For this reason, in Japan, it is traditionally believed that seated Zen meditation, in which breath control is important, is a way to self-regulation. Lack of self-regulation causes able people to fail to do as well as they are capable of doing in time of stress. When something important is at stake, people who have this emotional problem find that their muscles and their minds tense and prevent them from succeeding. No amount of consciously delivered advice can do anything about this, but breath control and reduced breath frequency can.

## (2) Rhythmical Breathing

Rhythm is as important to many aspects of daily life as it is to music. In sports, rhythm spells the difference between good and bad performance. For example, it is easy to tell the difference between skillful and poor swimmers by observing the rhythm of their actions. But the importance of rhythm is not limited to sports. In work, the man who establishes and adheres to his own rhythm of performance is likely to be more efficient and more successful than the man who works in a haphazard fashion. Our bodies themselves are governed by rhythmical cycles of actions; sleeping and waking are one of the most obvious. The functioning of the organs of the body—the heart, the lungs, and so· on—is smoother and the body is in better physical and mental condition when an innate, proper rhythm is maintained.

The measured rhythm of the way Zen priests chant the sutras is an interesting illustration of breath control used.to promote mental concentration. Of course, the texts themselves have deep meaning, but the rhythm of the chant plays an important part in this kind of religious observance.

The first step in developing rhythmical breathing is to select some phrase, piece of poetry, song, or any other kind of short text that you can repeat over and over in a fixed pattern. But it makes no difference what kind of rhythm one uses. It is important to select something that is pleasing. A favorite line from a poem or a song may serve this purpose. Language students might want to combine study with breath control by rhythmically chanting the conjugation of a verb. The key to success in this exercise is repetition. As you repeat aloud the words of the line or phrase you have chosen, in a rhythm that you find pleasing, your breath will gradually conform to that rhythm. Since you must repeat the phrase aloud slowly many times, this is not an exercise for the crowded commuter train. But you can find a few minutes a day, while walking along the street or while waiting for the train or the bus, to practice in a low voice that will not annoy the people around you. If you consciously concentrate on the rhythm of the thing you are repeating, your breathing will naturally fall in line with the rhythm.

As long as you concentrate on the rhythm of the words you are repeating, you do not need to worry about the length of exhalation and inhalation. These will take care of themselves; that is, as you say the words you will slowly exhale; and, at the rhythmical pauses in the text, you will naturally inhale as the air flows freely to the deepest parts of your lungs. This will naturally decrease the number of breaths each minute. This same effect can be produced by concentrating on a phrase or line that you repeat silently to yourself as long as it is done in a rhythmical way.

The method of reducing the number of breaths taken each minute and this rhythmical breathing method are similar in effects, though they differ in goals. Rhythmical breathing strives for concentration of thought; in addition, it is less concerned with great reduction in the number of breaths per minute than in the establishment of deep, regular, orderly breathing.

Everyone who has had to appear in a play or make a speech before an assembly has experienced stage fright: the cold sweats, irregular breathing, and rapid pulse that accompany the mild anxiety and the excitement preceding a performance. Some people, however, are unfortunate enough to suffer from this kind of condition in much severer degrees and much more often. Their pulse pounds, their breath becomes short, they break out in cold sweats, and they feel as if they were near death. In examining patients suffering from this condition, I have noted that they invariably breathe in a very shallow and irregular way when suffering an attack of what might be called an anxiety fit. Even when the fit has passed, however, shallow, irregular breathing persists; and one can never be certain that the tension the person is experiencing will not lead at once into another attack of severe suffering. People in this state of tension, manifest what I call unrhythmical breath.

The restoration of rhythm to the breathing by means of the exercise described here will calm the mind, remove anxiety, and enable even the timid to face his audience, his boss, or his new girlfriend with composure. In time of tension, the breathing becomes irregular. When one becomes aware of this irregularity, the tension increases; and this in turn further disturbs the breathing. But repetition of a phrase or song in an established rhythmical way restores order to the breath and in this way calms the mind and eases tension.

For people who find the other breathing exercises—for example the preceding reduction of the number of breaths taken each minute—difficult to master, I recommend the rhythmical breathing exercise. Often in the other exercises, distracting thoughts enter the mind and make it impossible to concentrate on breathing alone. In the rhythmical breathing exercise, on the other hand, the mind concentrates on the words being repeated; and the breathing regulates itself automatically. In this respect, it is the easiest aspect of Zen meditation to master.

## (3)   Abdominal Breathing

As should be clear by this time, breath control contributes to improved physical strength and mental stability. But there are many more methods for achieving this control than I have discussed yet. For instance, abdominal breath control is a system devised by the great Rinzai Zen priest Hakuin (1685–1768) on the basis of his own personal experiences. The characteristics of the system are these: the mind concentrates on the navel, the adbomen is tensed, and breathing is regulated. The method employed to achieve concentration in the navel is somewhat roundabout. If one sets out to concentrate one's attention on a certain place, like the navel, the result may be the development of sensations in that part that prevent the person from becoming as calm as he must. To avoid this, the Hakuin abdominal breathing method first required that you imagine a burning heat on the top of your head. The mind can concentrate on this imaginary sensation, and then this same concentration can be shifted to the navel or the abdominal region. Abdominal breathing counters the sensation of burning on the head. The theory on which this system is based is called concentration dispersal by psychiatrists and is related to the idea that excess concentration on one thing produces tension and is therefore negative in effect. Hakuin's theory, which is founded in modern scientific fact, has been of great value to medicine.

To master this method, first sit cross-legged on the floor with your hips pulled down to retract your abdomen. Your head must fall slightly so that your face is directed toward your navel. Your trunk leans forward slightly. It may be helpful to put a cushion under your buttocks. Imagine a burning sensation on the top of your head and breathe deeply and strongly to counter this unpleasantness. Once you have become accustomed to the method, simply assuming the cross-legged seated position will be sufficient to cause you to breathe slowly and deeply from the abdomen.

In order to discuss the reasons for the effectiveness of abdominal breathing, I must first mention the importance of the navel zone to proper functioning of the internal organs. Behind the stomach and below the navel is a network of autonomic nerves called the solar plexus, which controls the actions of blood vessels and capillaries that enable the liver, kidneys, and large intestine to remove waste products efficiently from the body and in this way to contribute to recovery from fatigue and to the creation of physical and mental strength to help the person withstand hardships.

It is undeniably true that the abdominal-breathing method, widely practiced by people who do not otherwise engage in Zen meditation, has been helpful in curing gastric ulcers, chronic constipation, and intercostal neuralgia in cases in which preliminary treatment and medication have proved futile. Falstaff in Shakespeare's *Henry IV* is an immense drinker and a glutton, but he is a man of humor and, above all, composure. Though it is not a good idea to copy Falstaff's bad traits, his better characteristics deserve emulation. And abdominal breathing can help generate calm and good humor in the face of irritations and difficulties.

Some simple animal experiments reveal the efficacy of tensing the abdomen in order to calm the brain and the body. For example, tapping a frog lightly two or three times on the abdomen will calm the flailing that the creature usually demonstrates as a result of fright at being captured. In my childhood, we often practiced hypnotizing chickens in this way. We would lay the bird on its back and tap its abdomen two or three times. For a short while, the bird would seem to fall asleep.

The parasympathetic nerves, which form a network in the lower part of body, are responsible for the constriction of the eye, the slowing of the heartbeat, and certain digestive functions. Stimulating these nerves—as it is possible to do by tapping a frog or a chicken on the abdomen—results in a condition resembling sleep. After-lunch drowsiness and total body relaxation are results of the stimulation of the central part of the parasympathetic nervous system.

Tensing the abdomen, as one does in abdominal breathing, re-presses the sympathetic nervous system, which, acting in opposition to the parasympathetic system, stimulates response to alarm by speeding the heart rate, raising the blood pressure, and so on. In other words, tensing the abdomen makes it possible to control the effects of the excitement-causing sympathetic nerves and to channel their effects indirectly toward the goal you have set for yourself. This enables you to remain calm in the face of danger and trouble. And this is the reason why abdominal breathing generates mental composure and enables you to make maximum use of your energy.

## (4) Counting Breaths

The breath-counting system is recommended to all Zen meditation beginners. It not only helps regulate the breath, but also provides spiritual unification. In other words, it is an excellent example of the Zen way of controlling the mind by regulating the outward forms and actions of the body. The simple system consists in counting silently from one to ten and inhaling deeply and exhaling slowly on each count. If it is done in the traditional Japanese cross-legged position, it is wise to use a cushion to prevent weariness of the legs. Sit with your back straight, your chin pulled in, and your tongue held against the roof of your mouth. Lightly close your eyes.

It is possible to practice this method of breath control while seated in a chair. With your back straight, sit so that your legs are moderately spread. Hold your hands, palms down, on your thighs. The fingers should be spread about equal distances. Direct your gaze to a position about one meter in front of you. When seen from the side, you will seem to have closed your eyes. This way of sitting —part of the Zen-meditation body-control method—will help you to maintain mental stability as you breathe to the count of from one to ten.

In the stress of modern living, mastering this exercise may be difficult because it calls for attention to be directed toward breathing, a part of our physical functioning that we ordinarily do not have to think about. This in turn may develop another kind of tension that must be overcome if breathing is to be controlled successfully. The Zen priests of the past always bathed or poured water over their bodies before beginning Zen meditation, and we today would do well to take this hint from our forebears. In addition to its hygenic aspects, bathing raises the body temperature, relieves muscular fatigue, removes stresses, and in general puts the mind and the body in good condition for breathing control. Four or five minutes of breath-control exercise after the bath is not too much time to take for the sake of the mastery of this important exercise.

My colleague and friend, Doctor Nobuo Takemura, of the Nihon

University Hospital, has proven the effectiveness of the breath-counting system in treating patients with neurotic symptoms. Of course, the breath-counting exercises cannot be used in initial stages of treatments. Before they can play their part in the cure, the patient's condition must improve to the state at which he no longer feels anxiety or emotional upset and at which his brain no longer emits predominantly active or tense beta waves. In other words, the patient must be at the stage of an ordinary person under moderate stress. At this time, however, the breath-counting system can contribute remarkably to further improvement in his condition.

Doctor Takemura measured the brain waves of neurotic patients undergoing breath-counting treatment and made the interesting discovery that their electroencephalograms display alpha waves at about the level of a person in the first stage of Zen meditation, though the patients' eyes are open throughout the exercise. Further, he discovered that they breathe at the rate of from six to nine breaths a minute, or about half the rate (eighteen breaths) for normal static conditions. Breath-counting exercises are the final stage preparatory to sending neurotic patients out into ordinary society again, free of unnecessary psychological stresses and ready to face life as a ship that has been in dock for repairs is ready to face the sea in completely seaworthy condition.

# 4. Mental Regulation

## (1) Concentration

In the preceding sections I have discussed ways to achieve stability by ordering the breathing and the body position. The use of control of the body to generate calm in the mind is a characteristic of Zen. In fact, Zen meditation is not considered truly effective unless it includes all three of these elements—breathing, posture, and mind —but all three are dealt with as an inseparable entity. I have shown how regulation of the breath and posture can have effects on the kinds of brain waves. But both of these phases are only external. They are comparable to building fine hospitals and filling them with therapeutic equipment, all of which is helpful but none of which can bring about a cure if the curative powers originating in the body itself are not stimulated. These inner powers are comparable to the strength to be derived from regulation of the mind.

Like regulation of breathing and body position, that of the mind can introduce much that is of value into daily life. The three practices together are of incomparable benefit; but, even if you have not mastered control of the breath and the body position, regulation of the mind can give you much wisdom that is of great value in daily activities.

The point of the mental-stability system is devising a way to control one's thoughts. From the viewpoint of neurophysiology, this means devising a way to convert tense beta brain waves into the alpha or theta waves that are emitted by a priest in Zen meditation. Dōgen called the state of mental control *hishiryo*. This somewhat difficult term means ultimate Zen enlightenment in some cases, but it also means the ability to concentrate the mind on one thing to the exclusion of all distractions. One must be able to concentrate in this way at any time and in any place. It is impossible for the human mind to remain completely without thinking for long times. On the other hand, too many small, unimportant thoughts can fill the mind to the extent that no meaningful thought takes place. *Hishiryo* is neither non-thought nor thought. It is both at the same time without being either. To think is to follow the proud notion that the thinking individual is the central being in the universe. The reverse of this is to feel inferior to all things. Neither of these approaches is consonant with the teachings of Buddhism. The state of *hishiryo* is thinking of nothing, not even of humility or virtue.

Although this might sound to abstruse to be related to our daily lives, such is not the case. People who are very good at some task, can accomplish large amounts of work efficiently and quickly while seemingly paying attention to everything else that goes on around them. Such people are not so entirely lost in their work that they lose sight of all other things. On the other hand, they are certainly giving their work thought. In fact they are concentrating on it while being aware of their surroundings. Their work apparently causes them little effort, though in fact it probably can be accomplished only at the cost of great diligence and perhaps suffering. This is true of great Zen priests, who remain silent on the subject of the intense introspective efforts they must make to achieve advanced mental states. Their brain waves, however, tell the full story.

The history of Japanese martial arts abounds in episodes of the superior awareness of people with developed abilities to concentrate while remaining sensitive to things taking place around them, but I shall content myself with telling only one. The famous swordsman Miyamoto Musashi once called at the home of a noted teacher of combat with the lance. At first there was some thought of the two men's engaging in a bout with the lance, but both soon realized that their would be no sense in such a thing. The lance teacher asked Miyamoto into his home and went out of the room on the pretext of preparing a special dish of food as a sign of his hospitality. During the father's absence, Miyamoto played a game of Japanese-style chess with the son of the household. Engrossed in the game, Miyamoto suddenly slapped a chess-piece on the board with a loud noise and shouted out angrily, "No you don't!" His young partner was startled at the outburst, but the game went on. It later turned out that at the moment when he shouted, Miyamoto, though apparently paying attention to nothing but the moves on the chess board, was aware that the head of the house was about to deliver a blow to his body from the neighboring room with a practice lance.

Before going on to the specific ways to develop this power of concentration-awareness, I must clarify one point. Zen concentration is not a way of foreseeing the future, though apparently miraculous tales like this one about Miyamoto Musashi seem to hint at supernatural powers. Because this concentration enables the person to be fully aware of his setting and of the actions happening in it, it seems to confer magical abilities on him; but this is not true.

Achieving the balanced state that is not thinking and not non-thinking but a balanced combination of the two is not easy; still, the Zen masters of the past have left the following method which helps generate a free and generous spirit. In modern psychological terms, the method may be analyzed into two states: concentration and contemplation. These are not two distinct states, but the early and later stages of the same method of mental regulation. Between the two are the transition and the association stages.

The kinds of concentration in which people generally engage may be classified as conscious or unconscious. Most intellectual activities, work, tests, or reading are examples of the conscious activity in which the individual deliberately turns his attention to one thing to the exclusion of all others. Willy-nilly, modern man is forced to do much concentration of this kind. Unconscious concentration or passive concentration, is a state into which the mind falls quickly because of long experience or training. In other words, the individual trains himself to concentrate his attention when he encounters a given set of circumstances. Ordinarily a person lives his life on no more than twenty percent of the memory and thought power he has built up during his past. In the state of unconscious concentration, however, it is possible to make use of from fifty to seventy percent of that memory and thought.

Concentration is simultaneously an end and a means. In the early stages, conscious concentration is a goal; but it later leads to a higher state. I shall begin my discussion with a method for achieving conscious concentration of the attention.

The state of *hishiryo*, or of concentration without thinking, is ideal; it is what is meant by Zen enlightenment. And from the standpoint of the modern psychologist, it is the state into which many neurotic patients must be led. In this state the individual is not obsessed with things; his mind is strong, free, and generous. And the strength of this state is what neurotic patients require to liberate themselves from obsessions with things and circumstances.

To concentrate, it would seem necessary to have something to concentrate on. On the other hand, I have said that one of the most important aspects of Zen meditation is that it does not involve obsession with things. This would seem to be a contradictory set of requirements, but it is not. As I have mentioned before, the desired state of concentration is one in which the individual is concentrating on something but is nonetheless aware of what is going on around him. To call again on the experiences of a famous swordsman, I mention Yagyu Munenori, who was once told something very important about concentration by the Zen priest Takuan Sōhō, who influenced both Yagyu and Miyamoto Musashi. In reply to the question of Yagyu about where one ought to concentrate when engaged in sword combat, the priest said that one must not concentrate one's spirit in any one place, for, if it is in no place, it can be in all places. Realizing that beginners cannot be expected to have sophisticated powers of concentration of this kind, priests have written many words of guidance on the subject. For instance, in one work by a priest who belonged to the Sōtō sect of Zen Buddhism it is said that, as a rule, during meditation, one concentrates on the hands. When one's mind sinks, it becomes necessary to concentrate on the top of the head or on the space between the eyebrows. When the thoughts ramble, one must concentrate on the abdomen; and when the mind seems to float unattached, one must concentrate on the feet.

But for the purposes of this book it makes no difference what you concentrate on. Select a crack in the wall in front of you. Or if one foot begins to hurt, concentrate on the other to relieve the pain. At first, your objects of concentration will change rapidly, but this does not matter.

It would be a grave mistake to assume, as some people do, that Zen meditation demands that one must never be sceptical or suffer. On the contrary, though the fixed, unwavering, unclouded mind is the ultimate goal, it cannot be reached without much perplexity and pain. Indeed Zen teaches that freedom from doubt is a sickness and that great enlightenment is born of great doubt. The way to overcome scepticism and suffering is to concentrate on them. To find the way out of the problem, Zen requires that one be thoroughly perplexed and that one suffer much.

The experiences of a noted Japanese author named Hyakuzō Kurata illustrate this principle. He was once much troubled with insomnia. He was unable to sleep for so long that the idea of being unable to sleep frightened him and aggravated his already sad condition. He found a way out of his suffering by requiring that he suffer more and by delving deeply into his own misery. Another case of a similar kind occurred when an executive in a certain company called on me to complain of being frightened by riding in automobiles that were descending a slope. His fear was so great that he had thought of resigning from his job, which entailed considerable travel to visit clients. After a number of psychiatric interviews with him, I learned that it was not automobiles or even slopes that disturbed him; it was the fear of moving from one place to another, the fear of seeing new locales and meeting new people. But I did not tell him this, for I realized that instead of pointing out to him the subconscious fear that was the true source of his trouble, I ought to encourage him to concentrate on his problem and in this way overcome it. My advice was that he never dawdle over work, that he immediately clean up any task he might have to do, and that he answer all correspondence at once. This would force him to face new things and to make new contacts through mail and other means of correspondence much more frequently than before. This would, I felt sure, bring the true nature of his problem to light and would relieve his suffering. I was right; in three or four months after he began following my advice, he started losing his fear of automobiles and slopes.

Zen teaches that one must not become obsessed with any one thing, but it also teaches another mental method in which one devotes all of one's attention to one thing. This method, called *zammai* in Japanese and *samādhi* in Sanskrit, is especially important for people who develop chronic instability and the inability to do any piece of work well because they can never resolve to devote themselves entirely to one thing. In an office, only a very skillful and experienced man can answer the telephone and do one or two other tasks at the same time. Answering the phone is a job that requires attention. Each of the other jobs that the skillful, trained man can do simultaneously requires complete attention of the less experienced personnel. Similarly, each kind of work demands the concentration of the people engaged in it. In other words, each job has its *samādhi*, or whole concentration. There is a *samādhi* for the technician, a *samādhi* for the office worker, and a *samādhi* for the housewife.

The former president of a famous Japanese newspaper tells how the advice of a kendo fencing teacher helped him improve his skill in this traditional Japanese martial art. It seems that this man, who had trained in kendo for years, made little progress because every time he began an attack to one part of his opponent's body he found himself hampered by the fear that he was leaving himself open to attack. When he consulted a kendo teacher who was also a practitioner of Zen meditation, he was told not to worry about being attacked but to concentrate on his own technique. He did this, and before long he found that he was doing much better. In other words, he concentrated on one thing at a time; he applied the rule of a *samādhi* for each action. This kind of Zen meditation enabled him to convert a fault into a merit. When a person is dissatisfied with a flaw and allows himself to neglect it and to be distracted by other things, the fault is likely to remain uncorrected. If that person concentrates on whatever is wrong with him, he will soon improve. This kind of concentration has certain defects. First, it tends to make a workhorse of the individual, who plods on concentrating first on one thing then on another. Second, it prevents the individual from being aware of everything occurring around him as he concentrates. In spite of these drawbacks, however, concentration is one stage through which everyone who practices Zen must pass.

And I have found that it is useful in psychotherapy. For instance, I have been called on for advice and help by housewives who complained that, once they were alone in the house in the morning, they could not seem to settle down to housework. These women were not especially busy; indeed they generally had more time on their hands than they could use effectively. By way of psychotherapy, I first asked them if there was not something of great importance that they knew they had to do. They usually replied that they did not know what that thing could be. I then told them that it was all right not to know but that they ought to give serious thought to their reason for not knowing. Most of these women, after thinking a few moments, came to the realization that they were not merely scatterbrained and unable to settle down to work, but were bored because all of their daily activities had become stereotyped. I then suggested that they try buying some new curtains or rearranging the furniture in the living room. Once they thought of some way to introduce variety into their lives, they usually found that their problem was solved.

The Rinzai sect long ago evolved a device for perfecting concentration in the priest and in the Zen practitioner. This device, known as the *kōan*, consists in statements given to student priests by their spiritual guide. These statements, or questions as is most often the case, cannot be answered by means of rational thought. They may involve knowledge that the student can have no way of obtaining. For instance, the *kōan* may be, "What did your mother and father look like before you were born?" or "What will the world be like after you are dead?" or "If you clap your hands together, which hand strikes the other first?" Apparently unanswerable, the *kōan* are issued by guiding priests to younger priests who are then instructed to meditate on them until they have arrived at an answer. The meditating priests are called one by one into the room of the guiding priest, who listens to the answers they have evolved through meditation. If the answer is satisfactory, the guiding priest says, "Good," If it is unsatisfactory, he says "No good," and the younger priest is instructed to return to the place of meditation and ponder the question further. This process may be repeated until the guiding priest is convinced that the younger man has a good answer or that he has been enlightened. When the meditating priests are inexperienced, they may be told "No good," many times indeed.

Obviously *kōan* like the ones I gave as examples cannot be in any sense answered by means of rational thought or the theories with which we are accustomed to solve problems in daily life. But because they demand concentration, for mental control, they are immensely superior to the system in which one chooses anything at hand for a topic of concentration and allows the mind to move from one subject to another. At the first stages of concentration on a *kōan*, it is necessary to employ conscious concentration of the attention. From this stage, one moves into a deeper state of concentration and hopefully to enlightenment.

*Kōan*, however, are difficult to use in ordinary life because they require the guidance of a priest who is experienced in Zen meditation and who can select the right *kōan* for the person and can understand whether that person's meditation is leading to enlightenment. But ordinary people can take advantage of the benefits of the *kōan* system. There are many kinds of topics that might be suitable as subjects for meditation: among the most psychologically useful are one's own weakness and faults. Ask yourself some of these questions as if they were Zen *kōan* to be pondered and answered in the most significant way possible: "How can I overcome my frailties and faults?" "Why am I weak?" "Why am I frightened when I must appear in front of people?" Everyone has some kind of weakness or fear: black cats or other things that, while insignificant in themselves, are sources of suffering for the person afraid of them. These matters involve emotions of embarrassment and shame that can make life gloomy and negative. By approaching them directly and meditating on them as if they were *kōan*, however, it is possible to solve the difficulties and bring light and activity into the life that was formerly made dark by weakness or fear.

The German psychiatrist A. Frankel gave the name "paradox intention" to a therapeutic system that resembles dealing with one's weaknesses by facing them frankly and meditating on them. The therapy consists of instructing people who have a fear to put themselves in a situation in which they must directly encounter the frightening thing or person. For instance, a person who is afraid of crowds will be requested to go to crowded places frequently. In this way, after a period of feeling abandoned by his doctor, the person comes to realize that he alone can solve his problem. And this is as good as being cured. Concentrating over and over on a thing—or coming into repeated contact with something, as in the case of this therapy—brings about unexpected developments in the human mind. Therefore, I insist that meditating on one's weakness and faults is an excellent way to strengthen one's personality. Furthermore, it is a method that can be used anywhere and at any time. Instead of fidgeting while waiting or dozing while riding the train, practice this kind of concentration for the mental benefits it will bring.

As should be apparent, the *kōan* is given to the trainee by the priest to enable him to reach the mental state of *samādhi*, which, requires the person to concentrate fully and to suffer fully in order to overcome suffering. Zen does not teach concentration so much as it teaches you how to give yourself perplexity as a way of controlling your mind. It teaches that you must inevitably experience the complexities and sorrows of human life. Obviously, knowing perplexity and suffering need not take the form of seated Zen meditation or the *kōan*; there are plenty of things in daily life that will provide chances to have this kind of Zen experience.

·A simple matter like making a purchase can show the advantages of being thoroughly perplexed and of confronting and overcoming the perplexing thing as one must in the case of the *kōan*. For example, imagine that you are trying to decide which of two articles to buy and you are utterly unable to come to a decision. Face the perplexity, wrestle with the decision, spend whatever amount of time is needed to come to your decision and you will always be satisfied with the purchase you make. If, on the other hand, you make a quick decision because the issue is too perplexing, you will always experience nagging doubts. You will never be convinced that you made the right choice. This is why I urge everyone, especially the impatient young, to be willing to confront perplexity in order to spare later regret.

As one repeats conscious methods for concentrating the attention and the mind, suddenly one becomes able to move unconsciously into a state of mental unification and concentration. The most important element in reaching this state is interest in everything around you and mental flexibility that makes all of the stimuli from the outside world clear and fresh. People who are deeply experienced in Zen meditation are rarely solemn or saintly in the conventional way. On the contrary, they are filled with bright interest in their surroundings. They are easily surprised. They laugh readily. And even people who have much less Zen experience than advanced priests say that, after a session of meditation, they hear and see everything with greater clarity and vividness. The green of the trees is greener and more beautiful; the songs of the birds are sweeter. During Zen meditation, as well, the sensory organs are extremely keen. An old Zen saying has it that the meditating man can hear the ashes fall in the nearby incense burner.

I have already said that unconscious concentration is the best kind. It cannot be summoned, for it would then ceases to be unconscious. To attain it, the person must be interested in and receptive to the object of that concentration. It is not unconscious when a person forces himself to concentrate on a distasteful piece of work or a difficult study assignment. On the other hand, the same person can concentrate completely unconsciously on some activity that he enjoys or is interested in. The way to develop control of the mind and to cultivate the power to concentrate unconsciously is to be interested in many things and to be receptive to many different kinds of stimuli. It is difficult to say whether the interest stimulates the sensitivity or whether the sensitivity produces the interest.

For the sake of learning how to develop a mind interested in many things it is helpful to try to find out why some things are uninteresting. Generally the causes of lack of interest are of one of the two following kinds. Either the thing in question fails to captivate, or it has become so familiar that it no longer awakens interest. There are two ways to overcome either of these failings in the object of your attention. Concentrate thoroughly and consciously in the way that I have described as being useful in overcoming troubles and difficulties. Or, if this does not produce the desired result, concentrate on the object with the intention of finding in it something, no matter how small, that is new and interesting. Looking for the interest or the beauty in something initially unattractive is by no means contrary to human nature.

Ever one has heard stories of people who have fallen passionately in love with persons who are far from physically lovely. The old saying that there is no accounting for tastes illustrates the complexity of human emotional responses and makes it clear that the human mind, if it concentrates, can find interest and charm in almost anything. Looking for the something new in a thing or person that has become too familiar and is therefore taken for granted is a somewhat different process. An experience related to me by a friend illustrates what I mean. On one occasion it was necessary for him to take a very early train from Nagoya in order to be on time for an important conference in Tokyo. Unfortunately, however, the train he was riding was delayed because of a malfunction. Unable to do anything to occupy himself and fretting because he would now miss the conference entirely, my friend sat gloomily staring out the window. Suddenly, however, something brilliantly and startlingly yellow flashed on his eye. It was a field of rape plants in blossom. Fields of this kind are not unusual on the route between Nagoya and Tokyo, and my friend had seen them so many times that he had stopped seeing them. But on this occasion, the color of the flowers seemed to be entirely new, fresher than he had ever seen it before. This newness in an old sight captivated him entirely. Engrossed in the scenery that he could enjoy as if for the first time, he barely noticed the passage of time. Before he realized it, the train was pulling into Tokyo Station.

This man was not practicing any of the concentration methods I have outlined as part of the Zen regimen for mental control. He had merely been surprised by something new in a familiar landscape, and the apparent novelty caused him to concentrate unconsciously on the scenery. It is true, however, that this particular person has the ability to discover interest where it might not ordinarily be expected. This ability has served him well in personal relations because he can find merit and value in most people. Unconscious concentration inspired by the ability to see the interesting in the things around you will help you live and work better with your fellow human beings.

**(2) Attention Transferal**

Everything that I have been saying about the psychological benefits of the state of concentration—especially unconscious concentration on an object—is true, but there is a point on which one must be very cautious. As the Chinese neo-Confucian philosopher Wang Yang-ming (1472–1529) said, being obsessed by a thing—love, money, or whatever else it may be—is to be a slave to that thing, to lose one's self. And this is not what is meant by the Zen state of meditative concentration called *samādhi*. This kind of obsession, or total concentration on one thing, causes the person to lose sight of all else. This is of course a kind of *samādhi*; furthermore it is something so entirely human as to preclude consideration of such value judgments as good or bad. But it is not the ideal Zen state because, as Wang Yang-ming noted, it is tantamount to slavery. If this is bad, what can be done about it?

It would seem that perhaps one way out of the dilemma is to keep a part of the self always awake and detached from the concentration process. But the tragedy of people who try to remain conscious and aware with one part of their self in order not to fall into irrational behavior is the condition called, in modern terms, schizophrenia. And one of the reasons for the popularity of Zen philosophy in the West is the power it has to cure the split in the self. The ideal Zen realm of thoughtlessness (*hishiryo*) has nothing to do with splitting the self.

Zen teaches naturalness and wholeness of the human heart. The concept of innate good and innate evil is Western; it is unrelated to Zen teachings, which profess the presence of the Buddha nature in all people. The object of Zen concentration is to manifest this Buddha nature by first training the mind to concentrate unconsciously on a fixed object and then gradually training it to concentrate on no fixed object. In modern cerebral physiological terms this means stimulating the brain to emit alpha waves in the meditation phase and then to continue emitting them after meditation has ceased.

To prevent the concentration of the mind in one direction and on one thing until a state of obsession develops, Zen teaches a method for changing the direction of concentration. This method is called the system for attention transferal.

The human mind is rarely as calm as an untroubled body of water. At almost all times, ripples or waves of pleasant or unpleasant emotion are disturbing its tranquility. Sometimes, the frequency of these disturbances reaches such a peak that the mind resembles a raging sea in which there is never an ebb tide to bring calm. The attention-transferal system can lower the frequency of disturbance and bring peace and a new emotional stability to the troubled mind.

The scholar or the novelist sometimes finds that his work has bogged down; he has concentrated so hard on his study or on his creative task that his mind no longer functions as it ought to do. A change is as good as a rest, as the proverb has it. And this is true. Getting away from a job that is no longer moving smoothly to think about something different for a while is an excellent way to restore stability to the mind and bring freshness to one's work. I am certain that this is too obvious to need explanation. The problem that remains to be solved is how to bring about this attention transferal. Probably every person has his own way of achieving the desired effect, but Zen has a built-in attention-transferal system that can be of help to everyone.

This method is divided into two phases: first, discovering what the thing that obsesses you is and, second, either performing a mental experiment to replace that thing with another or initiating a course of action at once. Some people may object that there is no need to find out what the obsessing factor is. It obsesses; therefore, its nature is obvious. But this is not necessarily true since the human mind often deceives itself by lying to cover up something that it does not want to recognize or to escape from something unpleasant. A simple example of the kind that we psychiatrists often encounter illustrates this point. There are neurotic people who complain that they do not like to go out on official errands or they do not like to attend conferences. But, put into positions in which neither of these apparently painful tasks is necessary, such people still do not lose their neuroses. The reason is that neither going out on errands nor attending conferences is the true cause of the trouble. The man who does not like to make trips out of the office is not afraid of the outdoors, he is shy of meeting other people. The person who does not like to attend conferences would love to be able to make brilliant suggestions at such meetings so that his talents could be recognized. but he is afraid that if he opens his mouth he will make a fool of himself. There are many people who think they are displeased, disturbed, or obsessed by one thing, when the trouble actually lies elsewhere. Some of these people turn to physicians, like me, for assistance when they could help themselves if they would only use their mind in the concentrated way prescribed by Zen mental control.

The basic nature of Zen meditation is a dialogue with the self: it provides a time of calm, undisturbed or distracted by thoughts, in which the individual can listen to the voice that is within. Immediately plunging into the bottom of one's mind, however is impossible; it is essential to sink gradually into the state of self-examination, constantly being aware of one's own mental and spiritual state. The Zen systems for controlling the breath and the posture are of great help in reaching deep levels of meditation. Humility and calm too assist in the descent into self-examination. Sometimes the mental sight of the true self and of the true state of affairs relating to the self is accompanied by intense pain. This is why the human mind often sets up self-defense systems or cheats in order to avoid inner scrutiny and thus spare itself suffering. But facing the truth and realizing one's true nature bring peace and calm to the mind. Running away from the truth cannot do this.

Once the truth has been seen and accepted, the person must not react in a negative way. The man who is afraid of conferences but who realizes that it is fear of mistakes, not of meetings, that upset him will do himself no good if he simply allows matters to remain unchanged and sinks into despondency over his ineptness. He must adopt a course of action to correct the failing that has been causing him trouble. He must transfer his attention away from his supposed inferiority.

Zen teaches that one must always be the master of the situation. I think this means that one must always be able to view the situation, including oneself, from the standpoint of the third person. This way of looking at things could very well help the man frightened of conferences to cure himself of his fears. He might do something like this. After setting up in his mind a kind of stage setting for a conference and determining who will be present and what topics they will discuss, he might run through a mental version of the entire meeting, question by question, remark by remark. He would try to find out not only what each person says, but also why. If one member of the group is the kind of person who attempts to silence opposition with sharp invective, he would try to discover the reason. Such a mental exercise will teach the man to see things from many different viewpoints. This in itself will prevent his mind from orientations in one direction and from obsessions. Repeated often enough, exercises in seeing things from various standpoints develop a mind that is able to switch easily from one thing to another. This in turn heightens work efficiency. For instance, people often claim that they cannot accomplish a task because too many unrelated thoughts distract them. The mind that is controlled can easily switch from a temporary distraction back to the job at hand.

I can summarize the Zen method for mental control, with the following list of major points. (1) First master the technique for concentration. (2) Then increase your concentration powers by moving from conscious concentration to unconscious concentration, thus learning to experience what is called *samādhi*. (3) To prevent being obsessed by one object of mental concentration to the exclusion of all other things, train to be able to switch your attention from one object to another.

The second phases of transferring attention and relieving oneself of obsession involves a course of deliberate action: face and overcome the thing that is frightening or obsessing by performing it. The man who is afraid of meeting people and of conferences ought to make as many new acquaintances as possible and attend as many meetings as he can. I once knew of a young man who was terrified of meeting people because he felt his manner of speech was awkward. He decided to overcome his handicap in the way I have described. Fond of collecting stamps, he often waited in long lines at the post office for the issue of special memorial sheets. During the time he spent waiting, he made a habit of talking to the people around him. Gradually, he found that people were not appalled by his manner of speech; indeed no one seemed to pay any attention to it. This gave him courage to continue the conversations. And, with each new encounter, he became surer of himself. He learned that not all people think his way and that most of the strangers he met were too occupied with their own affairs to be upset by his social awkwardness. By challenging his problem, he became master of the situation.

No matter whether it is achieved by means of the kind of mental experiment I described in the case of the man afraid of conferences or by means of challenge and direct action, the freedom to direct your attention and your mind as you wish will enable you to give fuller manifestation to your powers, to develop a more generous spirit, and to act freely and creatively.

### (3) Associational Method

Many people mistakenly think that in seated Zen meditation it is necessary to suppress the irrelevant thoughts that inevitably rise in the mind. This is by no means true. Drowsiness or slovenly posture are strictly forbidden, but irrelevant thoughts cannot be stopped; and the Zen method is to allow them to enter the mind as they will and to try to control them. Zen priests who have cooperated with men in electroencephalographic experiments have admitted that irrelevant thoughts occur and have insisted that they make no efforts to drive them from their minds. These thoughts usually form an associational series, which, when exhausted, fades, leaving the mind free to return to its concentration and meditation. For instance, one priest whom I interviewed related this series of thoughts. During meditation he heard the sound of someone's slippers in the corridor outside the room. This reminded him that his Zen master had said that quiet walking is essential in buildings where meditation is taking place. Lamenting that young priests no longer seem to take this kind of thing into consideration, the meditating priest decided that he must discipline his young charges. But this idea brought to mind a young priest who had been skillful at ringing the bell to call people to meditation. Next he returned to the problem of discipline, which he thought ought to be strict. The way in which one scolds, however, is important. Reflecting that discipline of young priests was his responsiblity, he remarked to himself that today people prefer gentle scolding. And, with this, the train of association faded.

A priest who cooperated with me in some of my experiments said that when distracting thoughts occurred to him during meditation, he made no deliberate attempts to drive them from his mind but waited until they left him on their own. He insists that the true meaning of Zen meditation is the spiritual unification that comes about as distracting outside thoughts depart, without the person's having been aware of their departure. Although there is always the danger that one will find oneself at the mercy of random thoughts, the characteristic of this phase of Zen spiritual and mental control is allowing the distracting thoughts to appear in the mind as they will and to establish the trains of associations that ultimately lead to the elimination of the distractions.

According to this discipline, one does not try to break the train of associations. Instead, one allows it to follow its own course until it ceases. If, for instance, something is on your mind and interrupts your thinking on another topic and in this way interferes with your work, you will probably only make matters worse by deliberately trying to forget the troublesome topic. The Zen way to deal with it is to think simultaneously about the topic and about your work or whatever activities you are engaged in at the moment. In this way you will set up trains of associations that lead to liberation from the thing obsessing you. Undeniably, thinking about outside things can have negative effects on your work and may cause you suffering, but Zen teaches that you must pass through the stage of distracting thoughts· and trains of mental associations before you can hope to enter the realm of tranquility and non-thought that is one of the goals of Zen and before you can devote your whole mind to one thing. Furthermore, miscellaneous and distracting trains of associations can led to solutions of problems. In other words, the distractions cease to be mere distractions and become one aspect of the situation requiring thought. The train-of-associations method, in short, is one in which you must concentrate on a single thing while giving thought to associative patterns about something else.

## (4) Meditation Contemplation

It is difficult to make a division between mere distracting, random thoughts and trains of association about them; both kinds of thought patterns manifest themselves at the same time, and one can be transformed into the other at the slightest stimulus. As I have said, Zen teaches that one must make no deliberate attempts to rid oneself of these thoughts and trains of associations but must allow them to flow freely. This leads to the fourth characteristic method of Zen spiritual control: meditative contemplation.

At the very mention of meditation and contemplation, modern people sometimes react by saying that they are too busy for such time-consuming activities, which are at any rate the proper province of religious seers and philosophers. From the scientific Zen standpoint, however, meditation and contemplation are not limited to certain intellectual types, nor are they the pastimes of the idle. They can be as important to health and well-being as sound sleep. I know that this is true because I have examined and tested experienced Zen priests in a state of contemplative meditation that allowed them to remain awake with open eyes and have found that at such times their brains emit the alpha waves that reveal a condition of mental calm and stability. Those of us who are not priests and who do not conduct regular sessions of Zen meditation must nonetheless emit alpha waves if we are to remain in good mental and physical condition.

Undeniably the modern way of living is busier and more frantic than the ways of life of the past. Even children must study, practice the piano, and do numerous other things that greatly reduce the amount of free time they have for play. The competitive nature of work in the adult world demands more and more time and energy output, and the pace of this way of life is affecting the lives of the young. It is frightening to think what kind of adults will result from a generation of children who have not known the free happiness of carefree play, of catching ball in a small garden, of laughing and talking in front of the television set, or of making model planes and boats.

Although adults constantly complain of the press of business, they seem to have ample time for leisure activities. Popular scenic zones are crowded throughout the year. And when the famous Japanese cherry trees bloom in the spring, they are almost overwhelmed by the long lines of automobiles of tourists out to enjoy the sight. Indeed, such conditions create the illusion that the cherries must flower solely to satisfy the demands of the tourists. This kind of illusion has come to be accepted as a reality, whereas the true reality is being forgotten and lost. Captured by the very idea of being busy, modern people fail to see the truth of the amount of time that is at their disposal. Parents who have lost sight of this truth force their children to live in the same frantic patterns of illusive busyness that they themselves follow. There are even those who attempt to deceive themselves and others about the true nature of free play and the role it plays by saying that leisure is part of work and that it is an extension of the tertiary industries. People who refuse to be deluded by the illusory reality proffered by such would-be deceivers are fortunate because they understand the meaning and value of play as play, not as a part of work.

What I have been saying about leisure and play makes it apparent that the individual ought to try to know the true reality within his heart. At the beginning of the novel *Die Aufzeichnungen des Malte Laurids Brigge* (*The Notes of Malte Laurids Brigge*) by the Austrian poet Rainer Maria Rilke, the hero makes a remark to the effect that, although the people around him seem to have come to live in the city, in fact they have come there to die. Whether Malte's interpretation of the urban way of living is correct or not, it tells us one important thing: we must not forget the reality that lies behind all illusions.

In order to survive in the modern world, the individual must take into consideration social common sense, the ideas that are current at the time, and the needs of social intercourse; but these things change rapidly. The consequence of the violent current of alteration in such issues causes each person to divide and vary his sense of values to meet the demands of the times. This in turn leads to a situation in which the individual loses sight of his own true inner values. Often awakening to loss of stable values occurs only late in life when the person, like Rip Van Winkle, opens his eyes to find everything and everyone around him aged and changed. When this kind of unfortunate person realizes that he no longer has values of his own, it is often too late for him to do anything about it. The contemplative method used in Zen meditation helps the person find his inner reality and, in spite of the turbulence and variety of daily life, enables him always to know what his self is.

Some scholars say that Zen is popular in Europe and the United States because it is difficult to attain mental stability and tranquility in the American or European way of life. Establishing the validity of this interpretation is a task beyond the scope of this book; but it is certainly true that people everywhere must not wait until economic, social, and other outside demands have blinded them to the nature of the inner reality. Since contemplative meditation helps the individual see this reality, I insist that it is for all persons and not for the philosopher and religious thinker alone.

Although contemplative meditation is one of the goals of seated meditation, one need not assume the traditional positions or conduct a course in Zen practices and training to engage in it. Since this, like all the other meditation methods I have explained, is based on the scientific truth of the teachings of Zen, it can become a part of the daily life of anyone.

The English word *meditate* is related to the word *reflect*, in the sense of reflecting on something. And all of the experienced Zen priests with whom I have discussed the matter agree that a state·of reflection—even in the physical sense of reflecting light—immediately precedes the state of enlightenment. Enlightenment may be compared to a smooth, unruffled, round basin of water reflecting outside things and occurrences with the clarity of a mirror. But should even a small thing—as small for instance as a tiny piece of ash from a stick of incense—fall into the water, a circular pattern of concentric-circular ripples expanding from the point of entry of the object, reaching the rim of the vessel, and returning to their center is set up. This pattern of waves crosses the water, strikes the wall of the basin, and returns, as if reflected, to the center. Without it, enlightenment in the true sense is impossible. In other words, though enlightenment is calm and static, it must be preceded by an active phase of reflection. Light striking the surface of a body of water disturbed by ripples is reflected in a highly complicated way from the horizontal, slanting, and vertical areas into which the action of the ripples divides it. Comparing the mind to this body of water, I can say that the ripples set up in the glassy surface correspond to the associational patterns of thinking, lead to a state of meditation that reveals inner truths, and in this way bring to the mind enlightenment on the subject of the meditation. Reflections from the many surfaces of the mind create a small universe.

Taking a concrete example based on the image of the mind as mirrorlike water in a container, I shall show how this works in contemplative meditation. Some stimulus disturbs the water. For instance, an attractive person passes by. The attractiveness of the person becomes a stimulus that interrupts the placidity of the water/mind and sets up outward moving ripples of thought: that is a good-looking person, I should take another look; but I will not. By this time, the thoughts have returned to the center to become another stimulus for a new series of thoughts beginning with something like this: why did I fail to take another look at that attractive person? These ripples will continue flowing outward and returning until the person is enlightened on his relation to attractive people, or perhaps on some other larger issue. This kind of meditation leads to the discovery of inner truths and to the placid, mirror state of enlightenment, which is, however, usually only temporary for some other stimulus is certain to disturb the calm almost at once. In other words, contemplative meditation is first the development of a mental idea about a certain stimulus. Then, the idea and the stimulus together give rise to another idea which demands comment or examination. As a result of the series of self-imposed questions and self-given answers on these ideas, the mind reaches a convincing conclusion on the issue at hand. Although this is relatively easy to explain verbally, it is much less easy to do. But if you persevere in examining your responses to stimuli in the fashion of the ripples moving from the center to the rim of the vessel of water and returning from the rim to the center again, you will gradually be able to employ the contemplative-meditation method whenever you like. The important thing is to use this method on every possible occasion.

None of us can see his physical form entirely at any given time. Similarly, though some people attain greater self-knowledge than others, few people ever attain entire enlightenment about themselves. When Hamlet says that there are more things in this world than are in Horatio's philosophy, possibly he is revealing his own intense self-knowledge. Though there are other people who, without fame or greatness, achieve the difficult goal of understanding what they are about, all too often, modern mankind fails to attempt intropsective examinations, probably, because we have all become too clever and too absorbed in superficial information. In spite of all the intellectual theories advanced today about the nature of the future, at no time in history has the future been more uncertain. To human beings who have lost the ability to examine their inner beings, I suggest the application of this method of contemplative meditation. Not only will it restore mental health and stimulate mental and spiritual growth, it will also help create a brighter future for humanity, since the human heart and its wholesome state are among the greatest treasures in the heritage of mankind.

FIG. 8 Group seated Zen meditation performed in a training hall together with a famous Zen master (on the far left). The training hall is part of a temple of the Sōtō Zen sect.

FIG. 9 This is a photograph of the same group shown in FIG. 8. The camera position was diagonally from the side.

# 5. Some Notes on Zen Training in Temples

During meditation sessions in training halls (FIGS. 8 and 9), a priest carrying a paddle called a *kyosaku* walks around observing the trainees and seeing whether their meditation positions are proper. When he finds a person whose position is wrong, he gently taps that person on the right shoulder with the *kyosaku* (FIGS. 10 and 11).

FIG. 10                    FIG. 11

FIGS. 10 AND 11   A Zen priest holding a *kyosaku* walks
quietly around the hall.

FIGS. 12, 13 AND 14   With the *kyosaku*, he lightly taps the shoulders of people who have become sleepy or whose attention has wandered.

FIG. 12

FIG. 13

FIG. 14

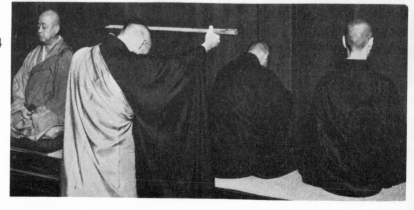

The person tapped raises his hands in the prayerful attitude and corrects his posture. Sometimes people who are strongly disturbed by various miscellaneous thoughts raise their hands together in the same way and lower their shoulders to indicate that they wish the priest to tap them on the shoulder as a way of ridding them of the disturbing thoughts (FIGS. 12, 13, and 14). There is a prescribed way of delivering the tap, and persons capable of performing this duty are generally mature in Zen meditation. Sleepiness, referred to as *konchin* (confusion) in Zen terminology, is strictly forbidden. The meditation posture of a person who is sleepy naturally becomes poor; consequently, the priest performing the task will tap him on the shoulder with the *kyosaku* to arouse him.

*Kinhin, or walking Zen meditation*: Sessions of orthodox seated Zen meditation usually last from thirty minutes to one hour. Priests may engage in more than ten such sessions each day.

FIGS. 15 AND 16   *Kinhin*, or walking meditation, is performed between sessions of seated meditation. A line, formed with the Zen master at the head, walks quietly around the training hall.

FIG. 15

Fig. 16

During the interims among them, they carry out what is called *kinhin*, or Zen meditation while walking (Figs. 15 and 16). During this kind of meditation, the arms are folded lightly on the chest, the body is held upright, and the feet are moved slowly along a straight line. In the very slow walking, one foot is advanced one-half step with one breath, then the other foot is advanced one-half step with the next breath. Figs. 17 and 18 show this in detail.

*Kinhin* has two major significances: it marks a division between longer sessions of seated meditation;.while providing brief repose, it enables the trainee to preserve the aftereffects of regulation over body, breathing, and mind and, in this way to make the next session of seated meditation more effective. In this way, it is a rational and scientifically based method for furthering maturity in meditation.

*Sesshin, or long-term Zen training: Sesshin* is an intensive week-long course of training conducted not only for priests, but for ordinary laymen as well. Its aim is to enable the trainees to attain the mental state known as *samādhi* or concentration. Usually held once in the winter and once in the summer, it need not be conducted at a temple.. Any quiet place where people can live together undisturbed is suitable. One Zen priest is the main guide. He is assisted by a number of other priests, all of whom devise ways to make the trainees' meditation deeper.

A typical daily schedule at a *sesshin* course is as follows. Trainees arise at five in the morning. After washing, they immediately engage in the early-morning meditation session (*gyōtenza*). This is followed by breakfast (*shukuza*) at six. Before the meal, such Buddhist

FIGS. 17 AND 18  Foot movement during *kinhin*, or walking meditation. On one breath, a half-step is taken forward. During the next breath, another half-step forward is taken on the other foot. The walking must be very slow and must be synchronized with the breathing. FIG. 17 was taken from the front, and FIG. 18 from the rear.

FIG. 17

FIG. 18

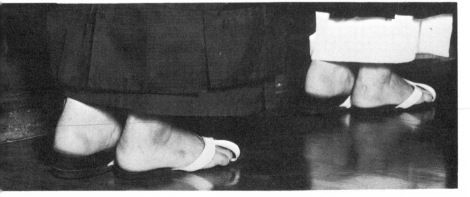

texts as the *Hannya-shin-kyō* (a one-page compendium of the *Prajñāpāramitā* literature) are read. Personal or random conversations are not permitted. For an hour or two after the meal, the trainees clean their rooms, the garden, and other parts of the building. Domestic work too is part of Zen practice. In other words, these activities deserve the same meticulous attention as meditation itself. From the time work is completed until noon, trainees engage in meditation—mid-morning meditation or *asaza* —interspersed with walking meditation. After the noon meal, which is conducted like the morning one, each trainee is given an hour of free time, though no one is allowed to leave the premises. Afternoon meditation (*hiruza*) continues from one to three in the afternoon and is followed by explanations of Zen texts conducted by leading priests. The choice of texts is up to the priest, but these difficult documents are explained in such a way as to deepen the effects of the trainees' meditation.

This session is followed by a brief (from fifteen to thirty minutes) rest during which the trainees are instructed in ways of adjusting their bodies for the next meditation session. This is followed by another meditation session, which lasts until five, when the evening meal is served. At this time, too, Buddhist texts are read or chanted. After the meal, each trainee quietly washes his own dishes. Even in connection with meals, they are not permitted to break the mood of Zen meditation.

After another intensive meditation session from six until ten (*yoruza*), the trainees bathe and go to bed.

Since this strict regimen continues daily for seven days, the people taking part in it—priests and laymen alike—must isolate themselves from the ordinary affairs of daily life. Furthermore, since all are equal before the Buddha, there are no distinctions on the basis of age, position, occupation, or sex, except that the sleeping quarters of men and women are separate.

The above is the standard outline for *sesshin* weeks, though, for the sake of enabling people to master or to deepen their own meditation methods, some variations are made according to the composition of the group of participants; that is, according to whether it consists of priests only, of laymen ònly, or of a mixture of the two.

Both Rinzai and Sōtō Zen strive to enable people to become mature in meditation, though in doing this, Sōtō makes fewer variations in the standard system. Rinzai, on the other hand makes extensive use of two devises not employed in the Sōtō sect.

Along with seated meditation (*shikantaza*), Rinzai uses the *kōan* and *sanzen*. The *kōan* is a kind of problem given by the Zen master to the disciple. (These are some examples of *kōan*. See or become *mu—mu* means nothingness. Hear the one hand clapping. What was your original countenance before the birth of your father and mother? When you are dead and cremated and when your ashes have been scattered, where will you be?) Many *kōan* of this kind have been prepared by famous Zen masters from ancient times. Each of them seems irrational and nonsensical.

*Sanzen* is the act of entering the room of the Zen master, alone, to state one's understanding of the *kōan* assigned. It takes place several times in a training day; and each time, the Zen master sternly orders the disciple to give his answers. In these sessions, the disciple's logical and dualistic way of thinking is relinquished, the double structure of subjectivity and objectivity is shattered; and, at last, the disciple attains a real awakening to his true self.

Approval of the trainee's solution to the *kōan* by the Zen master signifies that the trainee has experienced an awakening or self knowledge. This experience is called *kenshō*, and is considered proof of deepening meditation. The trainee is then assigned a more difficult *kōan*, the successful solution of which is another sign of self-understanding and deeper meditation. This method calls for giving the trainee a goal and forcing him to suffer through the solution of the irrational *kōan* and, in that way, to deepen his abilities in meditation.

Works by Japanese writers translated into foreign languages for the sake of explaining Zen to Westerners have dealt largely with the Rinzai sect. I do not claim that the many works written about the *kōan* and the *kenshō* experience are mistaken. I do think, however, that the attempt to bring about an alteration of awareness

—one of the major goals of Zen meditation—by the artificial means of the irrational *kōan* is unscientific. Though there were doubtless reasons why Rinzai believers did most to introduce Zen to the West,—this has brought about unfortunate misunderstandings. The English-language works of Daisetz Suzuki are a classical example of my meaning. Upon rereading his books, I was repelled by the way in which they treat, not the actual practice of Zen, but sophisticated explanations of Zen—oriental—philosophy and by the way in which they are divorced from reality.

Enlightenment is the central goal of Rinzai Zen; but, without Zen meditation practice, enlightenment is impossible to explain. The enlightenment that is taught by means of irrational *kōan* and emphasis on the *kenshō* experience is no more than a limited philosophical dogma.

Regulation of posture, breathing, and mind is the essence of Zen practice. Only through this kind of training is maturity in meditation possible. Enlightenment can be reached only as the result of accumulated experience and development in this kind of meditation. Meditation training that sets enlightenment as its initial goal is an artificial approach to the issue.

The kind of enlightenment taught in the books currently available to the people of the West is not the basic goal of Zen meditation. As I shall explain later, there is no scientific basis for the kind of enlightenment claimed for *kōan* and *kenshō* training. It is only a word used in imitation of Western rational thought and has nothing to do with true Zen meditation. The Rinzai process (*kōan—sanzen—kenshō*—enlightenment) distorts true Zen meditation and weakens its significance. Though some aristocrats or outstanding people of the past have attempted to attain enlightenment by means of the *kōan* process, such efforts are unrelated to Buddhist compassion. When such an approach to Zen was predominant, the true nature of Zen was lost. Today, however, Rinzai interpretations are losing ground because both the Japanese and people interested in Zen from other lands all over the world are demanding true Zen meditation.

# Psychophysiology of Zen

## 1. Scientific Basis of Zen Meditation

Not only people knowledgeable and experienced in Zen, but psychologists and psychiatrists as well have performed research proving that Zen meditation brings about an altered state of consciousness. But their work has relied largely on analysis of subject material related to them by the people meditating or on psychological tests given to those people. A number of considerations inspired us to want to provide a more objective scientific basis for the effects produced by Zen meditation.

In about 1955, we were performing measurements of brain waves by means of electroencephalograms—then recently developed—to examine altered states of consciousness produced by psychological disturbances. We learned that there is a close relation between these two things and between alterations in consciousness caused by alcoholic intoxication and addiction to sedatives and tranquilizers. But, though alterations in consciousness certainly occur during the periods of neurosis and psychosis of mentally ill individuals, scientific recording of such phenomena by means of encephalograms is very difficult. As we were desperately trying to find a way to understand the subtle changes occurring on the mental level at such times, articles written by two American research workers, Joe Kamiya and Charles T. Tart, shed light on our search. The work of Jaspers too stimulated us, as did the following remark by Carl Gustave Jung. (Indeed, this kind of remark was largely responsible for the increased interest shown by European psychologists in oriental meditation.)

"The eastern mind, however, has no difficulty in conceiving of a consciousness without an ego. Consciousness is deemed capable of transcending its ego condition; indeed, in its higher form, the ego disappears altogether."

Although I am not in complete agreement with Jung in general or with his antithetical stand toward psychoanalysis, this remark was a valuable supplement in our work on medical psychotherapy. In addition, we were influenced by the suggestion of Kanae Sakuma, whom I have discussed in some detail, that the key to the effect of Zen meditation might be found in brain waves.

## 2. Zen Meditation, Altered States of Consciousness, and Brain Waves

Brain waves, which are fluctuations of electrical potentials in the brain, can be measured by means of the electroencephalograph. These measurements make it possible to record characteristic wave-pattern curves from which to plot amplitudes and frequencies. In relation to normal wave patterns, it is possible to plot a number of electroencephalographic patterns.

Working on cats, H. H. Jasper showed the changes in brain wave patterns in the transition between waking and sleeping. The change between sleeping and waking, experienced daily by everyone is shown in the electroencephalogram. Other changes occur within sleep itself; for instance, fluctuation from shallow to deep slumber. And these alterations manifest themselves in the patterns produced by electroencephalograms. In deep sleep, the pattern is one of few waves with great amplitude (100 microvolts with a frequency of from 0.5 to 3 hertz). These are called delta waves. In a state of moderately deep sleep, rapid spindle waves appear in a mixture with theta waves, which have an amplitude of seventy microvolts and a frequency of from four to six hertz. Theta wave predominate in this condition. In shallow sleep, the so-called drowsy pattern is manifest; this pattern is characterized by irregular series of small-amplitude theta waves. Even a slight sound wakes a person in this state.

After H. H. Jasper, D. B. Linseley conducted further studies in which he combined the results óf research in brain waves during waking and sleep with his own studies of brain waves in connection with intellectual operations, emotional tension, and anxiety. As an outcome of this work, he discovered a continual fluctuation in wave patterns related to alterations of consciousness. This fluctuation is what he called the sleep-wakefulness continuum (FIG. 19). It is important to note that, in Linseley's patterns, alpha waves are not the stabilized pattern. It is generally accepted that electroencephalograms show steady alpha waves (usually about fifty microvolts and from ten to twelve hertz) when people are sitting calmly with eyes closed and that alpha waves do not appear in the brain wave patterns of people sitting calmly, but with eyes open. At such times, the waves are usually from twenty to thirty microvolts and have a frequency of from thirty to fifty hertz. This smaller, faster fluctuation is called a beta wave. Linseley describes the state represented by this pattern a condition of alertness. In daily life, the change from alpha to beta or gamma waves occurs in the form of a very fast alteration of consciousness.

FIG. 19 shows plottings of brain waves. Line A records brain

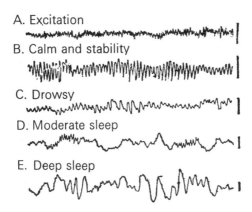

FIG. 19   Schematic representation of alterations in consciousness conditions as manifested in electroencephalograms.

waves emitted during ordinary mental activity. This pattern occurs generally when human beings have their eyes open. Line B shows wave patterns that occur in times of mental stability or relaxation. It is the first pattern to emerge in people engaging in Zen meditation. It occurs when the eyes are shut in ordinary people, though rarely in such a regular, typical form. The pattern in line C is that of a person who is drowsy but who can be awakened by a stimulus of some kind. The pattern in lines D and E are that of a person who has actually fallen asleep; the waves are low frequency: from 2 or 3 to 0.5 cycles a second.

In summary, this chart shows how brain waves slow down as the person moves from an active mental state to profound sleep and as the psychological system lowers.

## 3. Seated Zen Meditation and Brain Waves

FIG. 20   Collodion is used to attach the recording electrodes to the scalp.

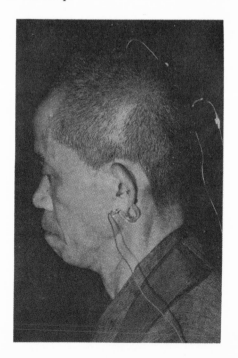

In this section, I shall discuss changes in brain-wave patterns brought about by seated Zen meditation. The discussion is made in the light of the hypothesis of Linseley and others.

In FIGS. 20, 21 and 22, priests are engaging in Zen meditation—both seated and walking forms. Attached to the head of each is an electrode for the sake of taking measurements of their brain

FIG. 21                              FIG. 22

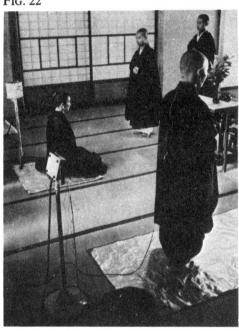

FIG. 21    Polygraphic recordings are made of the electro-encephalogram, pulse rate, respiratory rate, and galvanic skin responses.

FIG. 22    These experiments and recordings were continued for a week during an intensive training session (called *sesshin*). In this photograph, recordings are being taken from priests engaged in walking meditation.

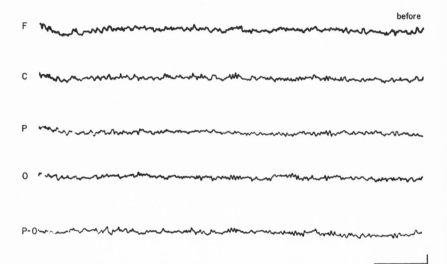

FIG. 23   Patterns recorded from a priest who was sitting with open eyes before meditation had begun. F, frontal; C, central; P, parietal; O, occipital region on the scalp midline. P–O indicates the parietooccipital bipolar lead. In this and the succeeding figures, calibration is 1 second and 50 $\mu$V.

waves. In our studies we found very little difference between the brain waves of priests in seated meditation and those meditating in the walking fashion.

FIG. 23 is the record of measurements made from a priest who now operates a Zen training hall in Paris for people of both sexes and all ages. The example shows brain-wave patterns for the time preceding a meditation session, during the session itself, and a period of forty minutes following the session. The letters F, C, O, and P indicate the part of the brain at which measurements were taken: F means the frontal lobe; C, the central lobe, which controls movement and emotional reactions; P, the parietal lobe, which integrates various sensory stimuli and issues commands to the other parts of the body; and O, the occipital lobe, which contains

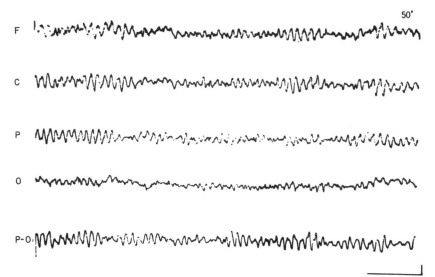

FIG. 24 Though the subject's eyes were open, well-syn-
chronized alpha waves (from forty to fifty $\mu$V)
appeared in all regions within fifty seconds of the
beginning of Zen meditation. The appearance of
alpha waves is less marked in the occipital region
than in the others regions.

elements controlling sight. The wave patterns of each part of the
brain vary slightly. P–O indicates measurements taken at a location between the parietal and occipital lobes.

At about fifty seconds after the beginning of the meditation
session, alpha waves are steadily being emitted (FIG. 24). The
priest's eyes were open at this time. At eight minutes and forty
seconds, the waves are slower than they were at fifty seconds after
the session started. They had been about ten cycles a second but
have decreased to eight. Since the priest's eyes were still open,
the chart for O, the occipital lobe, shows few clear alpha waves.
When the eyes are closed, the occipital lobe emits alpha waves,
while the frontal lobe does not. This is because the frontal lobe is
associated with creative thought processes and is so intimately.

connected with conscious mental activities that even closing the eyes does not affect it as quickly as it does the other parts of the brain. During Zen meditation, the cortex emits alpha waves first and with the greatest regularity.

At twenty-seven minutes and ten seconds after the initiation of meditation, theta waves have begun to appear (FIG. 25). These fairly regular waves of from six to seven cycles per second begin to emerge near the end of the meditation session. Even after the end of the session, the brain emits the kind of alpha waves that appeared fifty seconds after the session began. This classic example of a chart of brain waves is only one of many that we made on fifty-five Zen priests. From this considerable amount of experimental data, we reached the following conclusions.

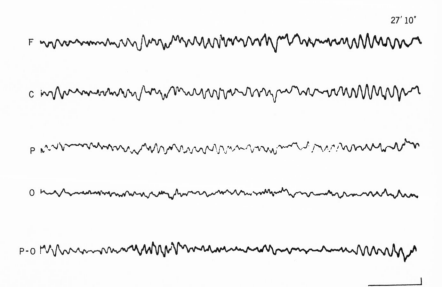

FIG. 25 Twenty-seven minutes and ten seconds after the beginning of Zen meditation, alpha waves (from seven to eight cycles a second) appear for one or two seconds in the frontal and central regions. After this, alpha-wave frequency decreases.

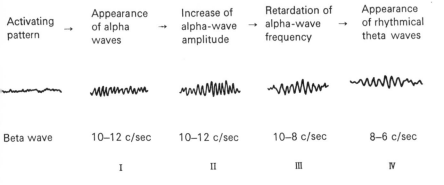

| Activating pattern → | Appearance of alpha waves | → | Increase of alpha-wave amplitude | → | Retardation of alpha-wave frequency | → | Appearance of rhythmical theta waves |
|---|---|---|---|---|---|---|---|
| Beta wave | 10–12 c/sec | | 10–12 c/sec | | 10–8 c/sec | | 8–6 c/sec |
| | I | | II | | III | | IV |

FIG. 26  Schematic representation of a series of electroencephalographic changes that occurred during a session of Zen meditation.

The stages of alteration of brain-wave emissions during seated Zen meditation are shown in FIG. 26, from left to right. In the first stage, alpha waves are emitted (Stage I); then the amplitude of the waves gradually increases (Stage II). Next the frequency of the waves decreases (Stage III), and finally theta waves begin to appear (Stage IV). An experienced Zen priest can enter Stage IV immediately after initiating meditation, whereas a very inexperienced person will be unable to progress beyond the first or second stages. In other words, level of experience in meditation, is to an extent revealed in brain-wave patterns.

In measurements of the brain waves of Rinzai Zen priests attempting to find answers to the *kōan* imposed on them by their superiors, we learned that Zen masters never accepted the answers of trainees who had been emitting beta waves at the time the solution was reached. To produce an answer acceptable to the master, the trainee had to reach Stage IV, or at least Stage III. This is an especially important finding, showing that in terms of the operations of the mind there is little difference between the training of Rinzai and Sōtō Zen.

FIG. 27 shows the effect produced on the brain waves by a sharp audiostimulation (delivered at the point marked with a C in the bottom line). At this time, for a while beta waves were emitted, but they soon gave way to another series of theta waves. When the sharp sound was repeated, the same thing happened. In some priests of high grade, this could be repeated with the same results over and over.

FIG. 27   Electroencephalographic changes that occurred in a Zen priest (forty-eight years old) during a meditation session. Rhythmical theta waves, appearing after the large alpha waves shown above, are blocked by a click stimulus.

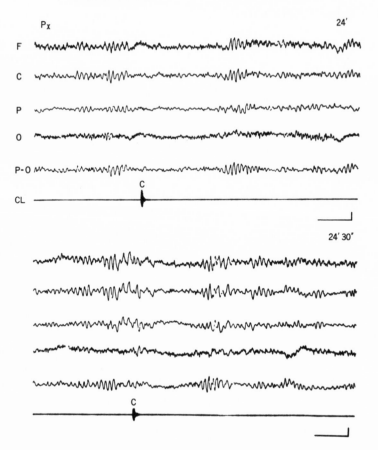

Sometimes, especially in concentrated, long training sessions, trainees become sleepy. FIG. 28 shows brain-wave patterns of a person sleeping during meditation. Although the patterns are not regular, in terms of frequency, the waves are identifiable as theta. They reveal patterns exactly like those of people actually in a state of light sleep. The pulse of the person measured in this case was slow, and his condition was that of a drowser. But, when a sharp audiostimulus was given (at point C), the brain stopped emitting theta waves and began emitting alpha waves.

FIG. 28   The drowsy pattern appearing in a Zen student turns into alpha waves at the click stimulus (C). An alpha-arousal reaction occurs. Key: RESP—respiration; SIG—signal of recording of clicks. The lower bank of readings is a continuation of the upper one.

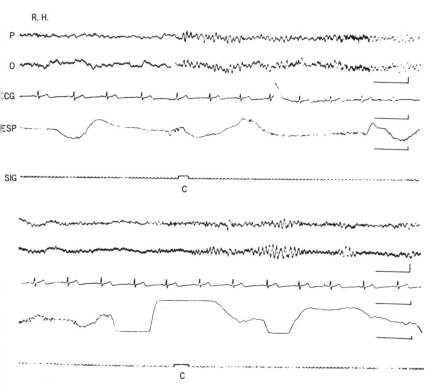

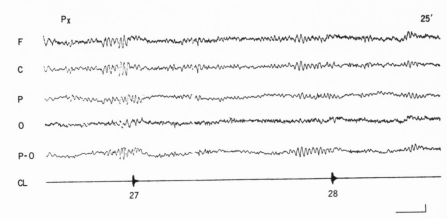

FIG. 29  The reading taken from a Zen monk who was sixty
years of age at the time reveals theta waves, sometimes blocked by click stimulus, during meditation.

The theta waves emitted during Zen meditation are more regular and their amplitudes are greater than theta waves seen in sleep. The important difference is the response to audiostimuli (FIG. 29). In the case of a person actually drowsing, such a stimulus causes the brain to emit alpha instead of theta waves. In the case of a person engaging in Zen meditation, however, the change is from theta to beta waves; that is, in the sleeper, the change is only one stage, though it is two stages in the case of the meditator. This seems to suggest that the brain operates in the same way as far as Stage III. The salient point is related to Stage IV. In both sleep and meditation, the brain drops to this stage, though the alteration is more sudden in the case of sleep. The sharp audiostimulus was a useful method in investigating the difference between the degree of drop in both instances.

The person meditating in the Zen fashion has his eyes open and is concentrating his attention inward. I had expected beta waves to predominate under these conditions, but my expectations proved wrong, for not the activitating beta, but the relaxed alpha and theta waves were conspicuous. When the meditator became slightly drowsy, theta waves appeared; but, at a clicking audiostimulus, theta waves were suppressed; beta waves emerged; and after one or two seconds, theta waves appeared again. A clicking sound causes a person who is drowsy or lightly asleep to cease emitting alpha waves, which do not recur thereafter.

In another experiment, we asked the head priest of a group to evaluate twenty-three other priests during a meditation session. At the same time, we measured the brain waves of the twenty-three men. Our results were arrive at in complete independence of the evaluations by the head priest; but, as FIG. 30 shows, there was a striking correlation between the stage of brain-wave patterns and his ranking. The vertical columns in the figure represent the head priest's categories: L for low, M for medium, and H for high. The dots indicate individual priests. All of the men except one ranked high by the head priest were in Stage IV of brain-wave patterns, and the single exception was in Stage III. Though the number of priests is not large, it is adequate for evaluation of brain waves during seated Zen meditation. We further investigated the relation between brain waves during meditation and the experience

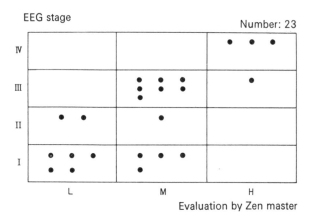

FIG. 30 Correlation between the electroencephalographic state of the Zen student (from I through IV) and the Zen master's evaluation of the quality of his meditation—Low, Medium, and High—at given times.

of the individual priests. Though the rate was somewhat lower than in the experiment on rankings, priests with more experience reached Stage IV more often.

Although it would seem that the state of the brain waves during seated Zen meditation is somewhere between that of tranquility and actual sleep, this is not always the case. Often the condition in meditation is unlike what happens under normal circumstances; that is, it is unlike the ordinary functioning of the brain.

The polygraph—sometimes called a lie-detector—is a device for recording galvanic skin responses (GSR), which are changes in the electrical resistance of the skin caused by agitation or excitement. We used such a device in an experiment designed further to study the nature of brain waves. A sharp audiostimulus was administered at point C in Fig. 31. This stimulus caused a peak fluctuation in the GSR reading. But immediately after it, and apparently the result of the influence of the same stimulus, there occurred a second peak. Like the first one, this one too was spontaneous. Ordinarily, response to stimuli in GSR takes from two or three to as much as six seconds to appear. In this case, however, the second peak appeared within three seconds after the first and was actually on top of the first. This heretofore unnoticed phenomenon indicates, not merely a lowered operation of the brain, but a heightened activity on the part of an undetermined function of the brain or of the autonomic nervous system.

Other unusual aspects of brain waves during meditation include lowering of the respiratory rate accompanied by an acceleration of the pulse and an absence of habituation to reduce or eliminate response to external stimuli. These findings suggest that Zen meditation is not merely a state between mental stability and sleep, but a condition in which the mind operates at the optimum. In this condition, the person is relaxed but ready to accept and to respond positively to any stimulus that may reach him. This in turn suggests that the operation of consciousness can be interpreted as an alteration of the brain waves.

Ordinarily, if the simple sharp audiostimulus is repeated often at a fixed interval, the meditating person whose eyes are closed

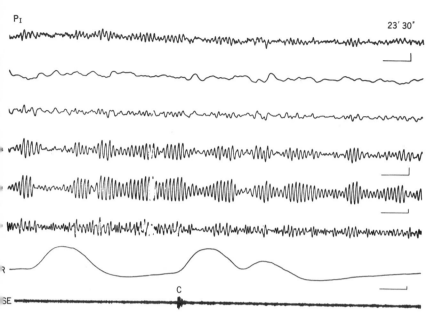

FIG. 31   In these readings taken during a meditation session
by a monk who was fifty-eight at the time, increases
occur in the alpha$_f$ and alpha$_s$ bands. The click
stimulus (C) provoked a galvanic skin response,
which was superimposed on the spontaneous one
for a short time.

becomes accustomed to it and no longer responds by emitting
alpha waves. The following experiment proved that the alpha rays
emitted by the brain of a person engaging in Zen meditation are
different from those of a person who is merely sitting with eyes
closed. We provided a clicking audiostimulus for four people who
were in the same room. Two of them were experienced Zen priests;
the others had no experience with Zen whatsoever. The results of
the experiment showed that, whereas ordinary people with eyes
closed become so accustomed to the clicking sound that they
gradually fail to react to it, Zen priests react unfailingly by altering
the kind of brain waves emitted at each new click, no matter how

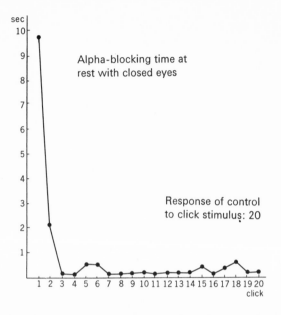

FIG. 32 Diagram of the alpha-blocking time for each click stimulation. The horizontal line represents the number of clicks repeated at regular intervals. In control subjects, the alpha-blocking time decreases rapidly after the fifth or sixth stimulus.

many times it is repeated. This suggests the existence of an optional excitatory state in the broad span of waking consciousness in the brain.

FIGS. 32 and 33 can be plotted of the changes caused in these charges by external stimuli. But, when a person is sleepy, the electrical charge of the skin decreases to such an extent that graphs of these changes become unplottable. In almost all cases, a click sound causes graphable fluctuations in the curves of charges when the alpha and theta brain waves were emitted by a person meditating in the Zen fashion. All of these findings show that the state of a person during Zen meditation is different from sleep and

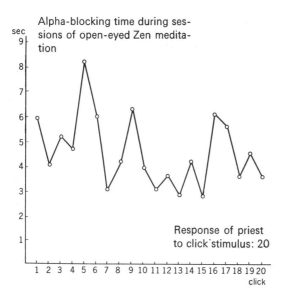

sec

Alpha-blocking time during sessions of open-eyed Zen meditation

Response of priest to click stimulus: 20

click

FIG. 33   In spite of some random fluctuations, alpha-blocking time remains constant.

that this difference is in fact the characteristic of the functions of the brain during such meditation.

# 4. Zen Meditation and Changes in Breathing

The chart in FIGS. 34, 35, and 36 shows changes in the breathing patterns of a Zen priest who was forty-five at the time of the investigation and who then had more than twenty years of experience in Zen. The upward curves represent inhalation; the downward ones, exhalation. The upper line is thoracic; and the lower one, abdominal breathing. In ordinary daily life, we breathe at a rate of about eighteen times a minute. Our breathing in such circumstances is largely thoracic. As this chart shows, before the initiation of Zen

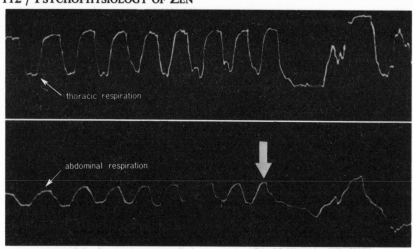

▲FIG. 34   Before meditation.

▼FIG. 35   During meditation.

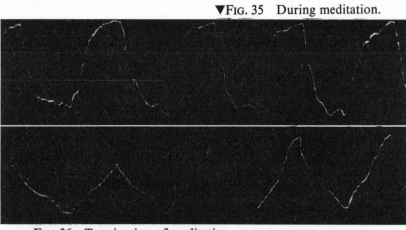

FIG. 36   Termination of meditation.

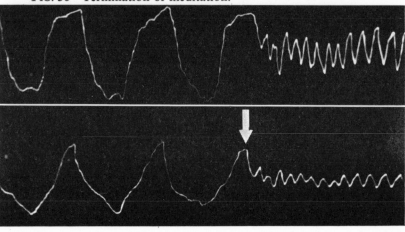

Figs. 34, 35, and 36  Diagram of the respiratory rate of a
monk before, during, and at the end of meditation.
The upper line represents thoracic, and the lower
abdominal respiration. Before meditation, the rate
is a normal seventeen or eighteen breaths a minute.
At the beginning of meditation (white arrow), the
rate decreases rapidly (Fig. 34) to remain at about
four or five breaths a minute throughout meditation
(Fig. 35). At the end of meditation (second white
arrow) the rate increases to twenty or twenty-two
breaths a minute (Fig. 36) but decreases to normal
before long.

meditation, the usual normal breathing pattern prevails. After the
initiation of meditation (arrow), however, the number of breaths
a minute rapidly drops to four or five. The fewer the breaths each
minute, the deeper and fuller they become. As meditation progresses, breathing becomes very deep; and the efficiency of the
lungs in taking in oxygen and ridding the body of carbon-dioxide
increases.

Following the conclusion of the meditation session (arrow), the
breath returns to normal, though, as in the case of this priest, it is
sometimes slightly faster than normal temporarily. Though his
normal rate is eighteen breaths a minute, after meditation, he
breathed at a rate of twenty-two breaths for four or five minutes
before returning to normal.

From general experience we know that, when the mind is at rest,
breathing tends to be more abdominal than thoracic. In meditation,
as time passes and as the breathing rate decelerates, abdominal
breathing comes to predominate over thoracic breathing. Although
investigations performed on twelve priests showed that not all of
them reached a low level of four or five breaths a minute and that
the more experienced the priest, the slower his breathing rate, all
of the men tested breathed much more slowly during meditation
than before it.

Professor Hiromoto Matsumoto, of the Komazawa University
Department of Psychology, after repeated experiments with the

Respiration of Zen master and monks during simple, quiet sitting and during Zen meditation (Matsumoto, 1970)

| Subjects (numbers in parentheses indicate years of Zen training) | A (30) | | B (2) | | C (11) | D (20) | | E (5) | |
|---|---|---|---|---|---|---|---|---|---|
| Experimental conditions | Quiet sitting | Zen meditation | Quiet sitting | Zen meditation | Zen meditation | Quiet sitting | Zen meditation | Quiet sitting | Zen meditation |
| Average rate per minute | 4.8 | 4.2 | 12.0 | 9.5 | 6.3 | 18.8 | 13.6 | 19.3 | 14.3 |
| Average respiratory cycle in seconds | 12.4 | 14.4 | 5.0 | 6.3 | 9.6 | 3.2 | 4.4 | 3.1 | 4.2 |
| Average inspiratory duration in seconds | 1.8 | 2.2 | 1.7 | 2.0 | 2.2 | 1.0 | 1.2 | 1.0 | 1.4 |
| Average expiratory duration in seconds | 10.6 | 12.2 | 3.3 | 4.3 | 7.4 | 2.2 | 3.2 | 2.1 | 2.8 |
| Standard deviation of respiratory cycle | 2.0 | 3.0 | 0.9 | 0.9 | 0.8 | 0.2 | 0.3 | 0.2 | 0.3 |
| Coefficients of variation of the respiratory cycle | 16.1 | 20.8 | 18.0 | 14.3 | 8.3 | 6.3 | 6.8 | 6.5 | 7.1 |

same results, showed that during Zen meditation the length of inhalation decreases on the average while the length of exhalation increases on the average. His findings offer scientific substantiation of the standard Zen-meditation training precept that all one needs to do to control breath is to lengthen the time of exhalation (Table). This tendency proved to be common among most priests and is illustrated by the smoothness of the exhalation curve in comparison with the inhalation curve.

A physiological investigation of the causes for these phenomena produced the following conclusions. First, it is a mistake to think of this breath control as a mere reduction of the number of breaths. As a result of the prolongation of the exhalation step of respiration, the deceleration amounts to an extension of the time of the entire breathing process. I have already pointed out the increased efficiency of oxygen and carbon-dioxide exchange inherent in this retardation. According to the findings of Hiromoto Matsumoto, whose work substantiates my own experimental conclusions and has great scientific significance, the physiological meaning of breath reduction is as follows.

If such a state exists during Zen meditation, it is natural that oxygen consumption should be lower on the pulmonary level. In other words, it seems likely that gases are exchanged in the lungs in the most effective way. At any rate, breath regulation does not mean hypoventilation.

The important point is that breath regulation does not cause hypoventilation, or insufficient oxygen in the blood. Although a number of research workers have reported that hypoventilation causes the brain to emit theta waves, as has been seen, reduction of the breathing rate does not bring about hypoventilation. This means that both phenomena must result from some distinctive physiological change brought on by Zen meditation in the functioning of the brain and lungs.

To prove this, we conducted an experiment in which we collected the exhaled breath of a group of priests in Douglas bags (FIGS. 37 and 38). Another experiment conducted according to the Douglas-bag method of Yasusaburo Sugi and Kunio Akutsu on a priest who was fifty-seven at the time and who then had about thirty years of Zen experience proved, as was expected, that the respiratory rate dropped dramatically after the beginning of meditation but that oxygen consumption dropped by from 20 to 30 percent of normal.

A combination of the results of this experiment by Sugi and Akutsu, the work of Hiromoto Matsumoto, and our own experimental results suggests that, as is the case with brain waves, Zen meditation causes certain distinctive changes. For instance, the reduction of the respiratory rate and the concomitant increase in total respiratory volume cannot be observed in any other condition. I have already shown that this state does not produce hypoventilation of the blood. To explain the mechanism connecting this with a sharp reduction of oxygen consumption demands an investigation of energy metabolism during Zen meditation.

Figs. 37 and 38   Investigations of tidal volume and oxygen consumption during Zen meditation. The Douglas-bag method is used to collect the total accumulated respiratory gas for the period of meditation. Gas analysis is then performed. This makes possible measurements of metabolic rates and of energy metabolism.

Fig. 37

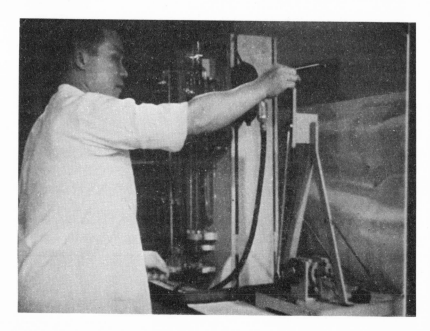

# Physiological Significance of Zen Meditation

Beginning five or six years after our work on the subject, a number of other specialists in the medical and psychological fields performed studies on changes in electroencephalograms occurring during Zen meditation. All of their results coincided with and substantiated ours. In the following section, I shall discuss research by others on aspects of Zen meditation other than electroencephalographic measurements. In all cases, the researchers were able to call on our measurements for amplification of their own psychophysiological studies.

## 1. Electromyograms

In 1962, Kenichi Takagi studied the effects of Zen meditation on various bodily functions in a Zen priest under conditions of normal (21 degrees centigrade), high (30 degrees centigrade), and low (16 degrees centigrade) room temperatures and learned the following. (1) Plethysmogram readings decrease during meditation, no matter what the room temperature. (2) Pulse waves on the plethysmograms do not fluctuate. (3) When the temperature was low (16 degrees), a slight increase of amplitude was observed. Takagi attributed this to the temperature. He confirmed our findings and those of Yasusaburo Sugi to the effect that a slight increase in respiratory rate occurs after the conclusion of the meditation session.

Sugi (1962) studied muscular reactions by means of electromyograms taken from a Zen student who was twenty-two years old at the time. During a meditation session, surface electrodes were attached to the following muscles on the young man's body: *M. rectus abdominis, M. sternocleidomastoideus, M. trapezius, M. latissimus dorsi, M. biceps brachii, M. triceps brachii, M. extensor digitorum communis,* and *M. flexor carpi radialis.* According to Sugi, the muscular contraction interval tends to lengthen as meditation time passes. For example, the contration interval of *M. extensor digitorum communis* is 1.83 seconds 5 minutes after the beginning of meditation, 2.23 seconds 20 minutes later, and 2.8 seconds after 40 minutes had passed. This kind of muscular relaxation during meditation agrees with knowledge gained from actual experience by Zen priests and with descriptions found in famous books on seated Zen meditation.

In studies on the relation between muscular relaxation and changes in electroencephalograms during the meditation of ten Sōtō Zen priests, Yukio Kambe and Koji Sato (1962) learned that the only relation between the two seems to be a decrease of discharges from *M. extensor digitorum communis* at the time when large alpha waves (70 microvolts in amplitude) occur on the electroencephalogram.

The meditation method used by a group known as Ishiguro Zen differs greatly from the traditional method and, as was reported by Yukiharu Akishige and his colleagues in 1963, produces different muscular reactions. Akishige discovered that, in Ishiguro Zen meditation, muscular tension decreases in the initial half of the session but that many muscular groups become excited in the second half.

Although R. Ikegami (1967) studied the significance of the full crossed-legs posture to changes in electromyography and found that this position was more stable than such other positions used by Zen priests as sitting cross-legged in the so-called Turkish fashion or kneeling with the back straight, he did not relate this stability to mental relaxation. It may be that the stability of the position is caused mainly by mental relaxation leading to the state of mind known as enlightenment, but further investigation of this subject is required.

## 2. Respiratory Functions

In 1958, A. Sakamoto reported that emotional excitement caused by efforts to solve *kōan* problems produces hyperventilation and increased respiratory rates during the early stage of meditation by priests of the Rinzai sect. As they become more experienced, however, these priests become able to exert voluntary control without emotional or volitional effort and thereby reduce their respiratory rates. Sakamoto further observed that, in states of mind like those attained by experienced Zen priests, breathing switches from thoracic to abdominal. He also investigated changes in the pH value of the blood on two Zen priests and showed that, during meditation, an alteration of 0.03 or 0.04 occurred, whereas no alteration at all occurred in the same period of time in the blood of controls who were not meditating. Sakamoto further noted a decrease in the amount of sodium bicarbonate in the blood of meditating priests and concluded that the decrease in pH value may be the outcome of voluntary control, through meditation, of the respiratory center.

In 1964, Yasusaburo Sugi and Kunio Akutsu measured changes in respiration and energy metabolism in twenty priests with from ten to twenty years' experience in Zen meditation. They learned that, during meditation, the breathing of such men was largely abdominal at a rate of from two to five breaths a minute and an average rate of four breaths a minute. Inhalation required five seconds; and exhalation, ten seconds or more. Though the volume of one exhalation may average as much as from 0.8 to 1.1 liters, the volume of ventilation may average as little as from 3.5 to 4.5 liters a minute. Using the Douglas-bag method, they learned that one minute after the initiation of meditation, oxygen consumption drops but remains at a fairly constant level thereafter throughout the session. After the conclusion of the meditation session, oxygen consumption recovers rapidly (FIG. 39). During the session, the rate of energy metabolism is from 75 to 95 percent (average 85 percent) of normal basic metabolism. During walking meditation, the rate is almost the same as that of normal metabolism. Sugi and

FIG. 39   Schematic representation of one monk's respiratory rate, tidal volume, and oxygen consumption. At the start of meditation, respiratory rate decreases sharply, while the tidal volume increases. During the full course of meditation, oxygen consumption dropped well below the normal level. Beginning and ending of meditation are indicated by arrows.

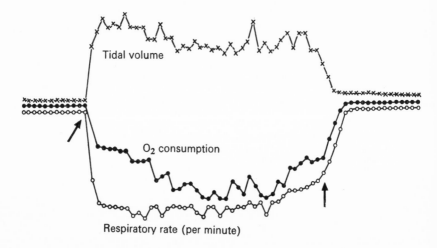

Tidal volume

O₂ consumption

Respiratory rate (per minute)

FIG. 40   Energy metabolism during Zen meditation. The line at the top indicates basic metabolism (which is assigned the value of one). The capital letters at the bottom of the column stand for the monks who were the subjects of this experiment.

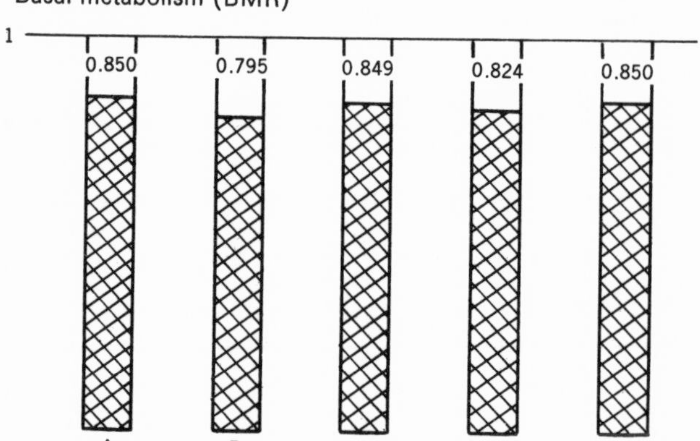

Basal metabolism (BMR)

1

| 0.850 | 0.795 | 0.849 | 0.824 | 0.850 |
| A | B | C | D | E |

Akutsu assumed that the marked decrease of energy metabolism is caused by a decrease in brain metabolism during Zen meditation (FIG. 40).

# 3. Galvanic Skin Responses

In tests conducted on twenty priests of the Sōtō Zen sect, all of whom had over ten years' experience with meditation, we learned that, during Zen meditation, galvanic skin responses are easily stimulated by an auditory click. As the meditator progresses through stages of change in electroencephalogram readings (stages I, II, III, and IV, discussed on p. 103), both spontaneous galvanic skin responses and those that are artificially induced by the clicking stimulus increases. The induced response often appears on the charts as superimposed on the spontaneous one. Repetition of the clicking sound does not dull reaction to it. Although Yukiharu Akishige has reported that Zen meditation suppresses responses to stimuli from within and without and that galvanic skin responses are lowered during meditation sessions, we feel that the priests on whom he conducted his experiments were less experienced than the ones with whom we worked and that this lack of experience may account for his findings. From our standpoint, changes in electroencephalogram readings are the criterion by which we judge a priest's training level in meditation; that is, the priest with more training emits theta waves sooner and more consistently.

# 4. Other Physiological Changes

The many physiological changes occurring during Zen meditation—especially in the bodies of well-trained persons—are believed to be completely nonvoluntary and often take place in functions controlled by the autonomic nervous system. As W. B. Cannon reported (1932), emotional stress of many kinds and the instinct of self-defense, when alarmed, cause reactions in which the predominance of the sympathetic nervous system is shown by increased oxygen consumption, hyperventilation, increases of blood pressure and pulse, and emotional stress. Cannon emphasized natural defense mechanisms and the role of the sympathicoadrenal system in homoeostasis (the maintenance of normal internal stability by means of coordinated responses of the organic systems that automatically compensate for environmental changes).

W. R. Hess, on the other hand, said (1962) that the motivation to achieve such equilibrium must be voluntary and conscious. In other words, a synergistic combination of conscious motivation working on the autonomic nervous system is operative in this situation. Hess proposes a mechanism in which one set of actions—he calls them *ergotropische*—operates on the external environment and another set—*endophylaktish-trophotrope*—operates on the internal being to maintain equilibrium. Equating his *ergotropische* with the sympathetic and *endophylaktish-trophotrope* with the parasympathetic nervous system actually oversimplifies the two concepts. It is wiser to say that these two opposing systems combine to maintain the cerebral organization and the integrated individuality. These now widespread views provide a basis for psychosomatic medicine.

In Western psychology and medicine, these systems are an explanation of the fundamental condition of stability and the various physiological arrangements made to restore the normal state when it has been disturbed. Cannon has said that the nervous system is divisible into two main parts: one acting outwardly and affecting the external world and the other acting inwardly, helping to preserve a constant, steady condition in the organism itself. Many Western scholars have identified the outwardly acting system, but the inwardly-operating one has long lacked a physiological basis resting on concrete evidence. In the East, however, scholars have found in Zen meditation an explanation of the physiological basis for the part of the nervous system that acts inwardly to preserve constant stability.

Zen meditation not only alters bodily functions, it also changes the conditions of the mind to enable the person to attain a kind of concentration (*samādhi*) through which he can reach Nirvana, or true enlightenment. According to Zen, Nirvana is the Buddha nature, which anyone can manifest if he will cease acting outwardly and attempting to affect the world around him. In other words, the Buddha nature is a constant, steady condition of the individual human being. According to many Buddhist writings, in latent form, the Buddha nature is unconsciousness in which the body and the mind are undifferentiated.

If this is true, it is only natural that Zen meditation alter both electroencephalogram findings and physiological functions like respiratory rate, energy metabolism, and galvanic skin reflexes. Later I shall deal with such questions as whether the mechanism producing physiological changes is natural and supported by the central nervous system. At this point, I should like to postulate a physiological basis for Zen meditation in terms of neurophysiology.

Concentrated Zen meditation, sustained by the deeper states of the human mind, decelerates brain waves. The electroencephalogram is based mainly upon the cortical potentials of the neocortex and its many neurons and synaptic reactions. According to Henri Gastaut (1945), in the ordinary waking state, cortical potentials maintain an activity level with a broad span of potential fluctuation. According to the activity level of the neuronal processes, in this state, electroencephalograms taken by way of the scalp show either the alpha or the beta pattern. During sleep, electroencephalograms reveal what is called the sleep pattern. Such neuronal processes result in the tone of the cortex (*Tonus corticale* of Bremmer, 1960). Deceleration of brain-wave frequencies as shown in electroencephalograms means a lowering of cortical excitatory state, as do changes during meditation as the meditator approaches the point where his brain emits theta waves. But the condition reflected by the electroencephalograms of a meditating person differs from both the normal waking and the sleeping states. It is a long-lasting, or tonic instead of phasic, change that is neither excitation nor suppression of cortical activity.

Whereas in the ordinary waking state, the cortex inhibits the activities of subcortical structures, during meditation there is interaction between the two. But, as the tone of the cortex lowers, the activities of the subcortical structures are increased by what is known as the release phenomenon. This leads naturally to hyperactivity in the autonomic nervous system, the functions of which are directed by subcortical structures. In short, alterations in galvanic skin reflexes, respiration rate, and other autonomic functions result from the release phenomenon at work on subcortical functions. Wolfgang Kretchmer postulated (1949) a deep person (*Tiefenperson*), which is a basic equilibrium between the conditions of the mind and the body. It may be that the mechanism producing the physiological changes observable during Zen meditation are similar to the mechanism of the *Tiefenperson*.

# 5. Voluntary Control

The numerous scholars—mainly American—who have worked on the subject have come to the conclusion that many involuntarily controlled functions, as an outcome of conditioned learning and trained effort, can be brought under voluntary control and oriented in a more wholesome direction (T. X. Barber et al., 1971). The desire to attain this end is the basis of mechanisms of voluntary control and biofeedback. In oriental cultural traditions, there are meditative exercises that, like Zen meditation, involve mental and physical homeostasis. Though the starting points of the study of American scholars working on voluntary control and biofeedback and of our own research differ, the aims and results of both efforts are the same.

# 6. Feedback Training and Voluntary Control

The interesting question of voluntary control of psychophysiological states cuts across several disciplines and cultural traditions.
In the future, issues of brain electrical activity, state of consciousness, psychosomatic effects, and meditation (in both Eastern and
Western senses) will probably become closely related to this
question.

Niele Miller and M. Banuazizi have performed experiments on
rats in which it was shown that functions controlled by the autonomic nervous system and therefore considered beyond voluntary
control can be trained to alter by stimulus and reward. On rats
paralyzed by means of curare and kept on artificial respiration,
they set up a system of electrical-current rewards that stimulated
the rats in some cases to alter the contraction rate of the intestines
and in other cases to alter the heart beat. In rats in which the reward
was directed toward intestinal contraction, no change was produced
in the heart beat, and vice versa. The altered rates continued for a
while after stimulus and reward ceased but gradually reverted to
somewhere near normal. This clearly proved that learning can occur
in such functions and that the learning is specific to a given organic
system. Though their work is concentrated largely on animals,
Miller and Banuazizi offer an interesting and valuable hypothesis
to the effect that drives and rewards induced by their method can
produce visceral learning serving to maintain homoeostasis.

Miller and L. V. DiCara (1968) assert the obvious functional
utility of learning during the process of mammalian evolution and
argue that functions subject to the control of the autonomic nervous
system are not directly subject to the learning process because they
do not exert a direct action on the external environment. They
further insist that homoeostatic regulation can be learned if a deviation from the optimum functional level occurs in the internal
organs to motivate such learning. Furthermore, the learning would
have to be reinforced by a reward—that is, a change in the direction
of return to optimum functional level—in order to be reinforced.

Whether or not this learning occurs depends on the possibility of deviations in functional level great enough to act as stimulating motivation.

Working over a number of years, Joe Kamiya and his colleagues have developed an experimental approach to investigating the relation between subjective experience and the electrical activity of the brain. Their method is to train people to discriminate among the kinds of waves being emitted by the brain at a given moment and to control changes in the kinds of waves. The subject sits with eyes closed in a dark room. When he hears a single ring of a bell, he is requested to say whether he thinks his brain is emitting alpha waves. He is informed of the accuracy of his answers. Gradually, he come to associate his own subjective experiences with the electrical activity of the brain and becomes accurate at saying whether or not he is emitting alpha waves. (This accuracy, of course, varies with the individual.) Finally, the subject becomes able to increase or decrease alpha-wave emissions—and thus to relax—voluntarily.

In later experiments, Kamiya abandoned discrimination training and employed auditory or visual stimuli that varied in intensity as the kind of brain waves emitted by the subject and recorded on the electroencephalogram varied. The auditory or visual stimuli were apparent to the subject; in other words, they were feedback information from his own experiences. It was learned that subjects who had mastered the training involved in this feedback system could control voluntarily the abundance of alpha waves and their frequencies, the abundance of theta waves, the location of the larger abundance of alpha waves between the hemispheres of the brain, left-right alpha dominance, and left-right alpha coherence. (Once again, there are differences in mastery among individuals.)

Words like *calm, relaxed, alert, and internally aware*, which are related most closely with the state of mind associated with consistent abundance of alpha-wave emission are similar to words characterizing the state of mind in Zen meditation when alpha waves are emitted with greatest abundance. As Kamiya says, feedback of the findings of electroencephalograms and consequent control of consciousness resemble the state of mind and the alteration in electro-encephalographic findings that occur during Zen meditation.

In the opinion of Elmer Green and others (1969), feedback from electroencephalograms employing a polygraph can alter the state of consciousness and produce a highly unusual state of mind in the subject. It seems likely that this highly unusual state is a unity in which the mind and the body are undifferentiated. Zen meditation, which, of course, is a religious self-discipline, can be interpreted in scientific terms as bringing about joint regulation of the mind and the body and thereby producing a psychophysiological equilibrium. It is, therefore, of great significance in connection with feedback and voluntary control. But there is an important set of differences between the two: Zen does not aim for learning as a reward, it is not a method of instrumental learning, and it requires none of the auditory or visual devices employed in feedback training. The psychophysiological state revealed by studies of feedback and voluntary control seems to exist within man. It exists also as part of Zen meditation. In our work, we attempt to bring into scientific focus the psychophysiological aspects of Zen meditation. Feedback and voluntary control methods in the West are scientific programs for the restoration of optimal psychophysiological health as well.

# Yoga and Hypnosis in Relation to Zen Meditation

## 1. Yoga

In studies employing electroencephalograms; electromyograms; skin-resistance tests; and measurements of skin temperature, blood pressure, breathing rate, and digital-blood volume during Yoga breathing exercises and the *samādhi*, or concentration, stage of Yoga meditation by 45 subjects in 98 sessions, B. Bagchi and M. Wenger (1957) learned that, in a few people, respiration rate dropped to from 4 to 6 breaths a minute (or shallow respiration for from 17 to 25 minutes) palmar electrical resistance increased (70 percent of the cases examined), and no changes occurred in basic electroencephalogram and electrocardiogram readings. They further observed spontaneous oscillation in the electrical-resistance line and sudden galvanic skin responses without external stimuli. The changes that took place in the electroencephalograph readings were the same as those observed in common sleep, or when alpha-pattern waves are being emitted during waking. In a few subjects, Bagchi and Wenger observed a period of more than twenty-five minutes during which low-intensity taps or noises within from three to five feet went unperceived by the subject. From these findings, they concluded that Yoga meditation entails deep relaxation of the autonomic nervous system and cerebral activity that does not produce highly accelerated electrophysiological manifestations and that involves varying degrees of insensibility to some outside stimuli for varying lengths of time.

The same ·researchers reported (1961) control of the heart in four Yoga subjects. Of the four, two claimed to be able to stop the heart and demonstrated how they did it, one made the same claim but only indicated his method, and the fourth claimed to be able only to slow the heart. The researchers concluded that the effects achieved by these men were the results of breath retention, considerable muscular tension in the abdomen and thorax, and a closed glottis (the Valsalva maneuver). They found that, though the heart did not actually stop beating in any of the four cases, venous return to it was retarded and pulse sounds either grew weak or became inaudible.

In 1969, Bagchi summarized the experimental findings in the following five points.

1. Yogi can voluntarily lower their metabolism rate for hours without going to sleep and can achieve much more than the normal rate reduction (from 10 to 15 percent) that occurs during sleep without producing hyperpnea or tachcardia.

2. Some Yogis manifest changes in such autonomic functions as palmar skin resistance and skin temperature. Bagchi calls these phenomena conditioned responses of the autonomic nervous system.

3. During Yoga meditation, brain waves are well-modulated and regular, like those occurring during mental relaxation.

4. In some Yogis, respiration tends to slow down; in others it remains normal. In the former group, the electroencephalogram does not produce a sloping pattern but remains in the·normal waking pattern.

5. Some Yogis claim to experience periods during which they do not perceive external stimuli. At such times, their electroencephalographs show only a slight shift of the base line, unaccompanied by blockage of the brain waves.

In spite of a Western tendency to confuse them, the trancelike state attained in Yoga and hypnosis can be clearly distinguished from the state of altered consciousness achieved during Zen meditation.

In my opinion, no one has yet succeeded in explaining the

hypnotic trance scientifically. Many have attempted to find a physiological index to differentiate the hypnotic trance from the waking state but have failed to do so. The various subtle signs—passivity, reticence, fixed facial expression, and so on—given as possible distinctions of the hypnotic trance necessarily differ with the subject who, in spite of similarity in reaction, may or may not have experienced an actual trance during the hypnosis session. In general, material on which estimations of the trance are based are verbal reports from subjects; and I believe that such reports alone are insufficient evidence. They must be substantiated by means of the application of some physiological index that correlates verbal reports with actual mental states.

The same thing is true of Yoga. So far, no physiological index has been found to certify in actual experience the claims made by Yogis concerning changes in such autonomic functions as heart beat. Wenger and Bagchi, who have done more research in Yoga meditation than any one else, suggest that the breathing and postural exercises common to some—thought not all—Yoga systems may be accompanied by significant autonomic changes and may thus give rise to enduring changes in autonomic equilibrium with possible beneficial effects on mental and physical health. The changes that occur in autonomic functions during Yoga may resemble those that take place during Zen meditation and may not yet have been observed in hypnotic trance states. There seem to be differences between autonomic functioning during Yoga and the same functioning during hypnotic trances, and I believe that the similarities between Zen meditation and some Yoga exercises are much less significant than the differences.

The religious goal of Yoga is union of the individual self with the universal, supreme reality. Through there are several Yoga systems for reaching this goal, the essential process in all systems is the attaining of a state called *samādhi*, or concentration, in which the person, no longer conscious of concentration itself, has, ostensibly, attained union with the universal. Not all of the people who style themselves Yogis have actually attained this state. Even the ones who have not reached the final goal, however, manage to discipline themselv.es and thereby produce changes in autonomic functioning that enable them to perform the amazing feats associated in the popular mind with Yoga. Strictly speaking, such changes do not seem to be an index of meditation or of attainment of *samādhi* but merely reflect alterations in bodily function produced by the different Yoga systems of practice. Before any definite conclusion can be drawn, scientific research must isolate the independent variables in individual kinds of Yoga practice and discover the common index in them all. Perhaps the changes produced by strict training—as.in Zen meditation—can lead to the ultimate state of *samādhi*, or enlightenment. Research workers interested in this subject and in so-called oriental mysticism should devote attention to a scientific examination of experiences common to Zen-and Yoga meditation.

Since there are many Yoga sects, it is necessary for the scientific investigator to select among them and to attempt to find true Yogis instead of people who merely pass themselves off as the genuine article. True Yogis are not always easy to locate, since they tend to live in retired, distant valleys, mountains, and villages of India, far from large urban centers. Differences in the Yogis used as subjects of scientific investigation often produce different experimental results. I have already outlined the work of Bagchi and Wenger in this field—they discovered changes in electroencephalograph readings and alterations in heart beat and respiratory rate. I shall now discuss the differing results of research conducted by Henry Gastaut and N. N. Das (1957) and B. K. Anand (1961).

Gastaut and Das report emission of alpha brain waves by Yogis who initiate closed-eye meditation—Zen meditation is always performed with the eyes open—and then attain the state of concentration known as *samādhi*. This state causes a desynchronization of fast waves (from forty to forty-five cycles per second), suggesting that the attention is focused on something. These findings differ from those of Bagchi and Wenger, who found a persistent, stable emission of alpha waves in such subjects. The discrepancy is perhaps accounted for by the fact that Gastaut and Das performed their experiments on Yogis from southern

Bengal and not, as is more common, on Yogis from the mountains of Kashmir. At any rate, because of this variance between two sets of results, it cannot be concluded that a desynchronization of alpha waves is a definite characteristic of Yoga meditation in general.

B. K. Anand working with Yogis in meditation and with Yogis who had attained a raised threshold of pain, discovered that meditating Yogis show a persistent emission of alpha waves of increased amplitude modulation that were not blocked by external stimuli during the *samādhi* state of concentration. In Yogis with elevated thresholds of pain, however, external stimuli failed to block emission of alpha waves. Anand and his colleagues showed that subjects who emitted distinct alpha waves in the normal resting period were more likely to persevere in Yoga training. They further claimed that there is no confirmation for the acceleration of alpha-wave emission reported by Das and Gastaut.

Though these findings correspond with the results of our experiments on Zen meditation in some respects, they are completely different in terms of reaction to external stimuli; it will be recalled that, in Zen meditation, all external stimuli produce reactions in the emission of brain waves and that the effect of the stimuli does not decrease with repetition. Generally speaking, however, in true Yoga, a pattern of well-modulated alpha waves persists uninterrupted by external stimuli throughout the course of meditation.

Gastaut and Das have stated that the pattern in brain waves produced by Zen meditation is unlike the persistent pattern produced by sleep or by the state of mind immediately following waking from deep sleep. Because the sleep pattern is characterized by persistent **slow** wave emissions unaffected by external stimuli, it is possible that there is some similarity between it and the state of concentration called *samādhi* in Yoga meditation, though there is no easy answer to this issue, which Gastaut ignores entirely. The same difference in reaction to external sound stimuli should remove the common Western misconception to the effect that the states attained by Zen and Yoga meditation are an identical kind of ecstasy. To repeat, results of electroencephalographic studies have proved that the two states are dissimilar. So far, research has not sufficiently clarified the relations between Yoga and Zen meditation and the states produced by the use of psychedelic drugs. It would be very interesting to know why some people are able to abandon the drugs by practicing Yoga. Electroencephalographic studies suggest that the effects of Yoga and psychedelic drugs on brain-wave patterns differ.

Whatever transcendental and mystical elements may be found in Yoga practices are different from concentration (*samādhi*) and are only means to a goal and not ends in themselves. The more highly refined techniques of Zen meditation naturally lead to the elevated state of mind that is enlightenment, or the Buddha nature.

The role of drugs in the ecstatic states of Yoga practice is interesting. According to K. T. Behanan (1959), most of the experiences of illusion and hallucination of Yogis may be traced to psychical causes, and there is satisfactory evidence to suggest that drugs may produce these causes. In the ancient Indian hymns mention is made of *soma*, an ecstasy-producing drug. Furthermore, even in the distant past, Yogis knew of the hallucinatory and ecstatic effects of certain drugs such as mescaline and hashish and made use of them in Yoga practices.

## 2. Hypnosis

Though no definite correlations between the hypnotic trance and electroencephalographic findings has been established, in 1968, P. London and his colleagues performed experiments showing that people who are highly susceptible to hypnotism generally emit alpha brain waves in large quantities. The failure of earlier researchers to discover differences in alpha-wave emissions between the waking and the hypnotic-trance states probably arises from the fact that these scientists performed their experiments on subjects highly susceptible to hypnotism and that such people tend to emit alpha waves even in the waking condition.

In our own experiments, we have discovered no definite changes in the electroencephalograph readings of people in hypnotic trance. Making measurements by way of the scalp, we found that hypnotized people emit few alpha waves and that the beta, or activating type, is more predominant than is the case in electro-encephalograms taken from people performing Zen meditation.

In research on the state he calls hypnotic sleep, Kiyoshi Fujisawa (1960) pointed out the emergence of a low-voltage pattern of theta waves similar to the ones occurring in drowsy people. These theta patterns persist as long as rapport is maintained with the hypnotized subject. But, once that rapport is lost, true sleep ensues.

In general, it can be said that, with the exception of the theta waves in the state called hypnotic sleep, no changes in electro-encephalograph readings take place during hypnosis.

In 1972, K. R. Wallace and C. Benson reported interesting tentative results on studies of physiological correlates in thirty-six people who had undergone short-term training in the transcendental meditation techniques developed by Maharishi Mahesh Yogi. These experiments revealed that, during such meditation, skin electrical resistance increases markedly, the heart rate decreases, oxygen consumption drops sharply—as was shown in our experiments on Zen meditation—carbon dioxide elimination increases, and lactate concentration in the blood clearly declines. Encephalograms showed marked increases and amplification of alpha waves in people meditating according to this system.

# Zen and Psychotherapy

Doctors and scientists in many parts of the world have found important psychotherapeutical applications for Zen meditation. In this chapter, I shall discuss the relations between Zen and a few psychotherapy systems.

## 1. Morita Therapy

Masatake Morita (1874–1938) developed a system of therapy designed to enable people to face their own anxieties and problems as part of the human condition. By becoming accustomed to problems in this way, subjects of the Morita method were able to live ordinary daily lives. The system, which in its original form contained no elements of Zen-like training or meditation, consists of four stages. In the first stage, the patient lies in bed for a week, doing nothing except facing his own worries, anxieties, phobias, hypochondrias, and obsessional compulsions. The second phase, which lasts another week, consists of light domestic work. The patient must carry out all assigned domestic tasks, no matter how apparently trivial or tiresome. In the third stage, which lasts for one or two weeks, the patient engages in heavy ordinary work and must keep his mind on actual objects. During these three stages, intellectual activity, reading, and pursuit of personal interests are forbidden, though the patient is requested to keep a diary. The fourth stage, a training period of from two to three weeks, prepares the patient to go into society and lead an ordinary life. All four stages are actually regarded as part of a unified whole, and their goal is to enable the patient to adopt a realistic viewpoint and to see his own sufferings, not as pathological symptoms, but as a condition existing in his own mind. As has been pointed out by J. Wendt, this system reflects the standard Japanese and oriental philosophical rejection of dualism of objectivity and subjectivity and actually contains nothing that could be called Zen Buddhist in the strict sense. Nonetheless, Naotake Shifuku (1972) sent questionnaires to twenty-five Zen priests, asking if they recognized relationships between Zen and the Morita therapeutic system. Twenty-two of the priests found similarities, and twenty-one of them admitted that the insight attained through the Morita system might have something in common with the enlightenment of Zen meditation. The methods of the two systems are, of course, entirely different. But C. Suzuki and Nobuo Takemura (1966) claimed good therapeutic results from an adaptation of the Morita system into which they introduced Zen meditation. This does not mean, however, that their modification of the original Morita system is a form of Zen meditation. Indeed, no definite relation between the two can be established.

## 2. Autogenic Training

The therapeutic values of the system of autogenic training evolved by Johannes H. Schultz, who published his book *Das Autogene Training*, in 1932, are widely recognized. The system involves six standard exercises and other meditative exercises based on the following three principles: reduction of exteroceptive and proprioceptive afferent stimulations, mental repetition of verbal formulas with psychophysiological implications, and passive concentration. Experiments indicate that passive concentration of the kind involved in autogenic training influences some autonomic functions: skin temperature, respiration, and electrocardiograph readings. The electroencephalograms of subjects who practice autogenic training for from two to four months show the pattern usually seen in predrowsiness; that is, anterior theta waves with a tendency to special generalization in the posterior regions and consistent alpha waves. Wolf Luthe concluded (1963) that regular autogenic training changes brain functioning at the corticodiencephalic level. Physiological changes in regular practitioners of autogenic training are similar to those that occur in Zen monks during meditation. For example, the retardation of the electroencephalogram pattern that occurs in autogenic training corresponds with what happens in our stage IV of Zen meditation. Nonetheless, the changes caused by autogenic training are apparently the result of alterations of autonomic functioning in the diencephalon, whereas those caused by Zen meditation are probably release phenomena caused by a decrease of the excitatory level of the cerebral cortex. In summarizing the results of his experimentation on this subject, Luthe said that the therapeutic key factor lies in the self-induced (autogenic) modification of the cortico-diencephalic interrelations that enable natural forces to regain their otherwise restricted capacity for self-regulatory normalization. Our work with Zen priests leads us to agree with this statement and to point out the great significance of the self-regulating normalization of these methods in helping human beings to rerealize natural forces. The true, deep human consciousness, which is never realized in daily life, can be actuated in such a way as to enable us to regain natural energies. Though his approach is that of psychotherapy for neurosis and ours is that of Zen meditation as conducted by normal Zen priests, Luthe's hypothesis and ours on this issue may coincide.

There are, however, significant differences between Zen meditation and autogenic training. Autogenic training teaches the achievement of reduced exteroceptive and proprioceptive afferent stimulations and the attainment of passive concentration by means of such repeated formulas as, "My arm is heavy, my arm is heavy, my arm is heavy." Zen meditation, employing no such verbal formulas, does not attempt to reduce external and internal stimulation within the mind itself. In autogenic training, the subject prepares a state of passive concentration by concentrating on first one then another of the peripheral parts of the body—"My arm is warm," "My leg is heavy," and so on. In Zen meditation, on the other hand, no such intervention of individual parts of the body is called into play. Though position and breath regulation are important, Zen meditation is internal control of the whole being without differentiation between the mind and the body.

Our experiments showing that repetition of internal and external stimuli does not produce habituation and a consequent dulling of response suggest that, even when passive concentration is prevalent in the priest's mind, an important element of active concentration is present and is under the control of the meditator. Yukiharu Akishige has said (1970) that active concentration is important to Zen meditation in order to prevent the meditator from falling asleep.

S. Nakamura investigated (1963) the possible psychophysiological effects that can be expected of Zen meditation, if it is truly similar to autogenic training, and came to the conclusion that, for the production of such effects, the self-control factor is essential. According to his experimental data, during Zen meditation, the cortical excitatory level lowers, and the autonomic nervous system is activated; whereas, in autogenic training, cortical functioning decreases and autonomic functioning relaxes. Nakamura suggests that the different self-control methods of the two systems may account for this difference.

# 3. Zen Meditation as Therapy

Research, stimulated by our findings on electroencephalograph readings, has suggested that there are mental and physical differences between Zen meditation and such systems as hypnosis (especially autohypnosis) and autogenic training and that autogenic training stands about midway between Zen meditation and psychoanalysis.

We agree with the opinion of S. Nakamura (1963), who has found that self-control factors, based mainly on physiological effects, are the principle reason for the effectiveness of a range of self-healing methods including Zen meditation, Yoga, autogenic training, Alexander's method, progressive relaxation, and so on. According to Nakamura, muscle control and breath regulation produce mental relaxation, which in turn results in external perceptual concentration, imagery concentration, and thought concentration. As the continued use of various self-control training methods for curing psychosomatic disorders indicates, man possesses self-healing powers that can be activated by such training. Psychophysiological studies of self-control or voluntary·control have given scientific evidence in favor of what I call the wisdom of the body. Zen meditation too produces physical and mental conditions that could contribute to mental health. It is not, however, used for therapeutic purposes because Zen meditation demands training that ordinary people. feel incapable of mastering and because it is basically a religious exercise aimed at the attainment of enlightenment as the paramount mental state.

Laymen in Japan sometimes turn to Zen temples for assistance in ridding themselves of neuroses. When meditation training fails to achieve the desired end, such people often become victims of what is called the Zen sickness. Though I do not think Zen meditation is in any way harmful to the mind, I do believe that the traditional methods of Zen training cannot have suitable therapeutical effects. If it is to be used as therapy, Zen meditation training must be changed. No efforts are being made in this direction at present. Most Japanese psychotherapists ignore the value of Zen meditation, though some physicians and scholars interested in psychosomatic medicine are beginning to turn their attention to this field.

In Zen training as represented by both the Rinzai and Sōtō sects there are two major aspects: spiritual exercises, including *kōan* and counseling sessions between master and trainee priest; and meditation. There is no clear dividing line between the two. Meditation produces the psychophysiological changes discussed in our experimental work with brain waves. The spiritual aspect of Zen relates to the meaning of psychotherapy. As Erich Fromm has commented, "...the knowledge of Zen, and a concern with it, can have a most fertile and clarifying influence on the theory and technique of psychoanalysis. Zen, different as it is in its method from psychoanalysis, can sharpen the focus, throw new light on the nature of insight and heighten the sense of what it is to see, what it is to be creative, what it is to overcome the affective contaminations and false intellectualizations which are the necessary results of experience based on the subject-object split." This is true, and Zen enlightenment may be a means toward insight in psychoanalysis. But this is unrelated to Zen meditation as a training method. As far as psychotherapy is concerned, Zen meditation resembles self-control, voluntary control, and autogenic training, all of which are based on common psychophysiological manifestatons. Zen spiritual training, on the other hand, may lead to the final goal of psychotherapy; that is, the discovery of the true self.

# Index